PRAISE FOR *YOU DON'T NEED AN MBA*

'In this moment, we need leaders more than ever. But, as Alicia McKay helps us understand, waiting two years for a piece of paper isn't required to make a difference. Start where you are and start now.'

Seth Godin, author of *This is Marketing*

'Credit belongs to Alicia because she is actually in the arena. Read this book if you want a down-to-earth, what-really-works guide to leadership.'

Greg McKeown, author of *Essentialism*

'McKay is right – you truly do not need an MBA or even an undergrad degree to succeed. What you do need is a structured way to think about building your career, and a good network. This book offers you an approach to building both that is practical and accessible. Most importantly, it's a fun read."

Kim Scott, author of *Just Work* and *Radical Candor*

'In *You Don't Need An MBA*, Alicia has deconstructed leadership to the point where it's easy to understand and action. Managers no longer have the excuse of not knowing how to step up – instead, they now have a choice. Read this book and grow… or don't, and become slowly irrelevant. It should be an easy choice to make.'

Colin D. Ellis, author of *Culture Hacks*

'If you want to master leadership and strategy, definitely don't do an MBA. Better to do what Alicia has done and spend two decades deeply immersed in the topic. Sift through the research; read hundreds of books, articles and white papers; think deeply on the topic, speak about it, write about it and teach it. In short, dedicate your life to it. Or, if you haven't got two decades, read this book. It has that very rare elegance and simplicity that only come on the other side of deep thought and hard work. And, as you would expect from Alicia, it's the antithesis of an MBA… accessible, quirky, moving, funny and, above all, practical and applicable. If you are in leadership, or aspire to be, this book should be at the very top of your list of recommended reading.'

Peter Cook, founder of The Expert Business

YOU DON'T NEED AN MBA

Leadership Lessons that Cut Through the Crap

Alicia McKay

MACMILLAN

For my three daughters,
Bailey, Charlotte, and Harriet –
the three strongest female characters I know.

First published in 2023 by Major Street Publishing Pty Ltd

First published in India 2023 by Macmillan
an imprint of Pan Macmillan Publishing India Private Limited
707 Kailash Building
26 K. G. Marg, New Delhi 110001
www.panmacmillan.co.in

Pan Macmillan, The Smithson, 6 Briset Street, Farringdon, London EC1M 5NR
Associated companies throughout the world
www.panmacmillan.com

ISBN 978-81-96365-33-2

1 3 5 7 9 8 6 4 2

Internal design by Production Works
Printed in India by Gopsons Papers Pvt. Ltd., Noida

SYLLABUS

MODULE 4: PERFORMANCE

MODULE 5: INFLUENCE

PREFACE

I'm used to seeing a raised eyebrow. I get it – it's triggering to be told how things work by some young upstart. While out for dinner with one of my biggest clients recently, I got the all-too-familiar third degree from his colleague. 'What qualifies you to do this? What's your background?' My client squirmed uncomfortably, mouthing 'sorry!' across the table when Mr Third Degree wasn't watching.

I wasn't bothered. Like many young female professionals, I'm used to it. Despite considerable advancements in diversity and inclusion and billion-dollar start-ups regularly being launched by 20-somethings, the preference for old white dudes with decades of experience prevails.

So before we go any further, let me be very clear about a few things:

- I'm not a former CEO.
- I don't have an MBA or a PhD.
- I'm not a white man over 50.

I am a facilitator, executive coach and corporate trainer who's worked with hundreds of senior leaders to make decisions and transform their lives and businesses. I've built my life, career and practice on strategy: thinking differently, making good choices and bringing change to life. With three kids to feed and without the comfort of secure employment to fall back on, I've learned fast and adapted quickly. I've had to stay impossibly attuned to the people who are trying to make a difference in government, business and their communities so that I know how best to help them.

In *Outliers*, Malcolm Gladwell states that mastering a skill takes an average of 10,000 hours of practice. I reckon I've got a few of those in my pocket:

- *Change* – The first 10,000. I grew up on a rollercoaster. In my 32 years, I've moved 34 times. A former foster kid, I had three kids by the age of 26, two of whom were born before and during my university years. I've moved cities, left jobs, started businesses and coped with parental abandonment, divorce, death, and just about everything in between. Change is my middle name, and starting over is my superpower.
- *Strategy* – Strategy is about working with what we've got to get where we want to go – whether that's personal or professional. It's about plotting a course of action that can withstand challenge, overcome constraints and engage the right people along the way. I started formally on this path as a policy advisor and strategic planner 10 years (and many more than 10,000 hours) ago, but I've been working around constraints to get things done for my entire life. From working out how to survive university as a single mother, to preparing business cases for large building projects or developing 10-year investment plans, solving tricky problems is my forte.
- *Leadership* – Over the last decade, I have lived and breathed support for executive leaders. Deep inside the teams, and heads, of people trying to make a difference, I've seen their frustrations and successes first-hand – including well-intentioned attempts at 'development' as they waded through the overwhelm. Passionate, dedicated leaders often find themselves putting in a second shift to invest in their own abilities, only to find themselves out of pocket and no better off.

In these 30,000+ hours of experience, I've noticed a few things. We've got some gaps – big ones. Stuff we don't spend enough time on in MBA courses or leadership development programmes. How to think, so that we can make good decisions. How to see the bigger picture, so we can bend and flex when our world changes. How to get things done and create something that matters. How to rally people to a cause, so we can have an impact at scale.

Baffled by these gaps, I've done the work. I've researched. I've tested my thinking with leaders and their teams. I've run workshops, held seminars, listened deeply – and I've got some ideas about what we should be investing in for the next wave of leaders.

Leaders like Mr Third Degree from the opening story are watching the sun set on their effectiveness. Steadfastly clinging to 'the way things are done' isn't serving them anymore. Their decades of experience and technical expertise are losing currency, and they're nervous.

They should be, too. The half-life of a skill has dropped from 30 years to just five. The skills and capabilities you need to do good work at the top aren't the same ones Mr Third Degree and his mates have been putting on their CVs for the last 20 years. They're certainly not the things you learn by devoting years of nights, weekends and lunchbreaks to an expensive MBA.

It happens to us all. We develop skills that serve us – until they don't. I'm as culpable as anyone, having lived on a steady diet of sheer grit and discipline for as long as I can remember. When everything was on fire around me, I kept working. A 5000-word essay due and a three-month-old baby that won't stop crying? No problem, I'll breastfeed while I pull an all-nighter. Family let me down? Water off a duck's back, I don't need anyone. Proposal rejected? Great, I've got six more in the pipeline. Divorced and starting from nothing? I'll take a deep breath and build it all again.

None of this was to impress anyone, but to prove to myself that I could; to sate my appetite for safety and control, after an early life that lacked both. Unfortunately, that appetite made me an insufferable control freak, and the cracks started to emerge – tiny ones at first, but they got bigger quickly. In the last year, I've been dodging signals from every angle – my children, therapist, coach, friends – even my body! A twinge at the gym damaged the rotator cuff in my right shoulder recently, leaving me unable to write, type or lift – or whiteboard – for weeks. My coach wryly observed, 'Your right arm? Do you think that's a coincidence? Are you going to listen yet?'

So, while our journeys might be different, we're all on one. When you've been rewarded for being busy and for your capacity to know and deliver, you work on those skills and structure your life around them. The idea that doing more of that isn't going to get you any further is scary.

I'm scared, too. Like many people, my frame on what mattered changed in 2020. I am learning that I can't run my practice or my family, or be happy, by continuing to do everything myself. I can't get better by doing *more of the same*; I have to do things *differently*. Ironically, this is what I've been preaching and supporting others with for years. It is precisely my area of expertise: strategy, change and continuous transformation. I've worked with hundreds of senior leaders, facilitated more than a thousand workshops and implemented dozens of change processes. I've sat alongside people struggling to come to terms with what their new future might be – but it's hard to practise what you preach. It's the same reason the builder's house is never finished, and the accountant's budget is a mess. I know now that my potential is limited by my own work ethic.

Doubling down on a skill you've been rewarded for makes logical sense – until that overinvestment starts to cloud your judgement and hold you back. For enthusiastic doers, a narrow emphasis on delivering can come at the expense of big-picture progress and new ideas. For deep thinkers, having your head in the clouds and over-analysing everything can leave you stuck and frustrated. For bands, every album can start to sound the same. And just like people who need to shift the way they live and work, change carries the risk and the fear of losing everything they've built along the way.

Moving ahead sometimes means having the courage to let go of old ways of working, old relationships and old skills.

On the speaking circuit, we often see the 'I almost died but didn't' speaker, who built their profile on a near-death experience. They spend as many years as possible milking it, telling the same story and trying to draw new lessons from it, but they're not growing or adapting enough to leave that crutch behind. I see leaders that do the same thing.

Maybe they pulled off something amazing, and now they're trying to coast on it for the rest of their career; or perhaps they're in a sector that plays chief-executive swapsies, so they think they're set for life. They've dedicated their life to tracking up the ladder and reckon if they keep doing more of the same, they're safe.

Those leaders are in for a nasty shock. Overreliance on any one thing is bad practice – and it's a risk that seems perfectly safe until the day it gets you. Unless you diversify your strengths, that thing will inevitably stop serving you. Eventually, it may even be what brings you down.

Our leaders' ability to cope with constant, daily change has never been more important or poorly understood. The world keeps throwing curveballs, and it's easy to get overwhelmed. It's not that we don't know we need to change; the gap isn't knowing, it's doing. The leaders of tomorrow need to change today. They need to get smart, be strategic about the next step and expand their range to face a complex and uncertain future. They need paradox: clear values and open minds, high performance and meaningful space, dedication to detail and big-picture perspective. They need to ask different questions, design different options and most of all, they need to do that with others on the same journey.

The good thing is that these are first-world problems with first-world advantages. We face these challenges while sitting in expensive offices, using incredible pieces of technology and with some of the greatest productivity advances in the world at our fingertips. We're figuring out how to collaborate while communicating at the touch of a button, and we rarely stop to think about how we'll pay our mortgage or feed our kids.

But despite these incredible advantages, we're burning out. Even with time-saving tools and technologies on our desk, the expectations on our time and energy exceed our capacity. We're tired, stressed, pulled in a dozen different directions – and we're not taught how to do things any differently. Instead, we're quietly encouraged to keep pedalling. We talk a big game about space, presence and systems change, but our expectations and behaviours don't match up. Even the most forward-thinking and strategic leaders I work with are oppressed by a cult of busyness, nervous about proving their worth ahead of an ever-impending restructure and desperate to show how invaluable they are.

If you feel this way, you're not alone. The incessant expectation of busyness doesn't discriminate by title, sector, gender or specialty. Whether you're in corporate, government or non-profit, chances are you're losing your shit for half of every week.

I see you; I am you, and I can help you. Every day I work with leaders who recognise that the things that got them this far are now holding them back. Every day I work with leaders who gently tilt their axis in another direction, and I see first-hand the difference it makes. I watch detail-oriented thinkers become thoughtful strategists, frustrated introverts become influential experts, and exhausted heroes design and delegate to powerful systems.

That's not to say it's easy. Going against the grain never has been. It is powerful to recognise that what's great about you is also what's holding you back. Committing to a new way of being, even though it won't be a smooth journey and you'll repeatedly and visibly mess things up, needs strength and vulnerability in equally large doses.

But it's worth doing. Becoming a strategic, intentional leader won't just serve you at work. You can draw on this skillset every time you face conflict and change, every time you confront something about yourself that you don't appreciate, every time you have to make a tough decision or put aside your fears or ego to do something important. Every time your values are challenged, and you have an uncomfortable feeling in your gut about the right choice, you can draw on these skills.

In this book, I'm going to outline a different path to the classic MBA. There's no corporate finance or heavy textbook here. Instead, I'm offering you a level up – in how you think, what you see, how you act and what you get done. A new way of thinking about leadership. I'm not asking you to tap into your strengths and get better at what you already do; I'm asking you to put some of that down, and stretch in a new and uncomfortable direction.

Let's be clear though: you're already awesome. You wouldn't have picked up a book on strategic leadership if you didn't have the basics on lock. You wouldn't be questioning your abilities or asking bigger questions if you didn't realise that what you're doing isn't working any more. And you wouldn't bother reading this if the challenges you're facing weren't significant.

I'm not promising transformation, or that every answer you need lies within these pages. But I can promise to open your mind to something new and help you start to stretch.

I hope you agree and disagree with me in equal measure. I hope you shake your head violently and exclaim 'YES!' – on the same page. I hope you email me with your thoughts, post positive and negative comments on social media and start a conversation based on the ideas you find here. I hope you share this book – dog-eared and scribbled in – with your colleagues, friends and teammates. I hope you still get an MBA, if you want one – but that you look at it with different eyes.

I hope you reference some of these ideas in conversation and that something you read resonates. I don't care if you remember where you heard it, just that you did. Most importantly, I hope you try something new to see if it works and keep looking for opportunities to do so.

Go on, get out there. I'm with you.

A

INTRODUCTION

> *Here lies Alicia. She sent many emails and wrote many reports. Long live her memory.*

How's that for an epitaph?

> *When I grow up, I want to answer emails.*

… said no-one ever.

> *Woman consistently achieves performance targets.*

… doesn't make the newspapers.

At the beginning of strategy or coaching sessions, I regularly ask senior leaders the same question: 'what's your job?'

People always tell me the same things. Their job is to 'navigate the future', 'empower their teams', 'make things happen', 'make progress through change' and 'serve their customers and community.' But when I ask to see their calendars, my request is often met with an uncomfortable squirm. It's not that we don't *know* what we're here for; it's that what we're doing doesn't quite line up.

The way we spend our time and energy rarely matches our priorities. Thanks to the relentless march of business-as-usual, our most meaningful work gets squeezed around the cracks of urgent issues, meetings, emails, approvals and minutiae.

As Mark Manson once tweeted: 'What gets attention is rarely important. And what is important rarely gets attention'.

Leadership is a privilege. When people trust you to steer a team, family or community, you hold something special in your hands. If that's you, take a moment to be thankful. I know the responsibility is heavy, but the opportunity to do meaningful work that positively impacts others is an incredible gift. People all over the world are battling for survival and yearning for meaning, and you get to shape your own life and help others. How good is that?

It's easy to forget this when we're wrapped up in the daily grind. An anecdote from Donald Miller in his book *A Million Miles in a Thousand Years* has always stayed with me. Imagine, Miller muses, that we head to the cinema to watch a movie about a man who wants to buy a Volvo. After working for years to achieve his goal, he finally drives his car off the lot, testing the window wipers as he goes. Is this a beautiful movie you'd tell your friends about? A hero's journey that would leave you in tears? Of course not. Odds are, you wouldn't even stay until the end. Yet, as Donald says, we spend years living stories like these – working every waking moment, accumulating stuff we don't need – and expect our lives to be meaningful. The truth is, as he says:

> *If what we choose to do with our lives won't make a story meaningful, it won't make a life meaningful either.*

Life is full of high-pressure goals that are the equivalent of a Volvo. Calendars are packed with back-to-back Volvo acquisition strategy sessions, which then trickle down into our to-do lists. If we're not careful, the Volvos start to make us numb. They tire us, frustrate us and consume our energy – and then stasis sets in. All the joy and potential seen in our thankful moments seem miles away when we're jamming 80 hours of stuff into a 40-hour container. Over time, the Volvos start to erode our sense of purpose. We get disenchanted and disengaged. We stop trying to make things better or pushing for change because it feels futile.

Strategic leadership rises above the Volvos.

Without the skills to cope with the hard stuff, we manage our overwhelm by busying ourselves. Being busy is reassuring, easy to do and rewarded. We're never short of things that require attention. Who has time to navel-gaze about the future or contemplate the nuances of change when there's so much to be done?

But managing overwhelm with action placates us with a false sense of achievement, while we slide invisibly backwards. With every email answered and every report written, we fall deeper into mediocrity and denial. Failing to adapt, we become less and less relevant – and our opportunity for meaningful contribution moves further out of reach. But it doesn't have to.

History is littered with examples of leaders who found purpose through madness. As Britain faced a Nazi onslaught in World War II, Prime Minister Winston Churchill rallied a country behind him. Katharine Graham, leader of the *Washington Post* in the 1970s, stared down political pressure to publish the Pentagon Papers, exposing the reality of the Vietnam War and drawing a line in the sand for independent journalists the world over. Polar explorer Ernest Shackleton led a pioneering expedition to Antarctica, holding his team together in an incredible survival story against all the odds.

You might not be leading an expedition or steering a country through crisis, but the lessons are the same. If the world around you is going mad, you face an opportunity to shape your leadership in a way that matters.

Change and complexity isn't a distraction from the real work. It *is* the real work. Leaders are made, not born. No-one arrives ready to cope with complexity – they develop those skills inside the madness. And no-one becomes a great leader without them.

ON COMPLEXITY

Work feels less knowable than it used to. Our parents and grandparents left school, got a job or looked after the kids, and felt confident doing that work until retirement. It wasn't necessarily easy, but it felt stable.

Teachers taught. Lawyers lawyered. Doctors doctored. Mechanics fixed cars. Kids learned, from school and at home, what work was all about. They picked a path and off they went. But now, when my kids talk about what they want to be when they grow up, I'm not sure what to tell them. What is a teacher in pandemic uncertainty and with online learning? What are lawyers as we advance blockchain, encrypted data and global commerce? How will medicine evolve as bedside assistants become robots, society ages, the middle class questions vaccines and biotechnology hurtles ahead? What knowledge, if any, will you need to fix a car as we shift towards multimodal transport, automated vehicles and sustainable energy?

According to a LinkedIn source, people will, on average, switch jobs fifteen times in their lifetime, which could include a handful of significant career shifts. Change is not new. We've been grappling with new occupations, ideas and technologies since forever. But the kind of change we're dealing with is different now. Like our career paths, it feels less knowable than before. Things are more *complex.*

We need to be careful with words like 'complex' because, like 'leadership', it falls into jargon territory. For the purposes of this book, here's what you need to know about complexity: it's more than just complicated.

Practically speaking, the main difference between 'complexity' and 'complicated' is that when things are complicated, we can usually work out what will happen – if we know the starting conditions. Complicated problems are tricky, but they're solvable with the right rules, systems and processes. The electrical grid is complicated: there are many possible interactions, but they follow a pattern. Because of those patterns, we can make accurate predictions about how the system will behave. Flying a commercial aeroplane has lots of complicated steps, but they're also predictable, and as a result, it's astonishingly safe to do.

So, while complicated situations might involve lots of different people and considerations, we can predict how they'll interact. These situations are knowable. Complexity is not. It's uncertain, ambiguous and unpredictable. In a complex system, the same starting conditions can produce different outcomes every time. Flying a plane is complicated, but air traffic control is *complex*, thanks to constant changes in weather, aircraft downtime and other variables. Air traffic control has been shaped into a manageable system not because we can predict what will happen, but because it's designed to adjust continuously.

Complicated situations have lots of moving parts, but they can be untangled and sorted out. With complexity, the same variables interact in unpredictable ways, creating disproportionate and unexpected consequences.

The world of work, and indeed the world itself, has become a more complex system. There are lots of moving parts – people, technology, environment and money – and we don't know what's going to happen next. Instead of treating our jobs like flying a plane, we need to be more like air traffic control. We can't predict the future, or control the outcomes, so we need to build our capacity for responsive, continuous change.

ENTER THE ARENA

Fiction writers often talk about the difference between plot-driven and character-driven stories. In *plot-driven* stories, like mystery novels, the story is shaped by action and conflict, as we follow the twists and turns, leading to an eventual reveal. The reader is consumed with piecing together plot points and ideas, while character development takes a back seat.

In *character-driven* stories, the focus is on the inner conflict of the people involved, usually centred on one main protagonist. We invest in the characters, follow their journey and connect with who they are, what they think, the decisions they make and how they evolve.

When management and leadership science first took off, our focus was on plot. In the 1980s and '90s we were largely transactional, sharpening up operations and management. It was all about measurable, orchestrated action. In the New Zealand public sector reforms of the 1990s, five-year chief executives replaced permanent heads of department, and the relationship between policy and delivery teams narrowed to outputs, contracts and deliverables. Leaders were encouraged to sharpen their pencils, specify KPIs and hold people accountable.

In contrast, most of today's leadership theory is about character. Focusing on attributes and behaviours, we describe the kind of person you need to be and the kind of people you need to hire to succeed. Tools like DISC or Myers-Briggs categorise traits, strengths and personality quirks, hoping to order a complex human system into a suite of snappy acronyms. Leaders learn they've got a red dot, a blue aura, a dove communication style and were born as a XYZ personality type – and they are encouraged to build teams with the right combinations to match.

A third and lesser-known fiction format is the *arena-driven* story. In arena-driven stories, the environment is a critical antagonist for our characters, shaping the challenges they face and the journey they travel. In stories like *Cast Away, Gilligan's Island* and *Lost,* the main character survives a difficult environment, which drives individual choices and overall results. Here, the emphasis is less on character and more on context: the complex, interconnected environment that demands response and adaptation.

Nothing we do is independent of our context, and this is where traditional leadership theories often fail. They offer a step-by-step guide to behaviours that makes plenty of sense – until you get back to your desk, something changes and it all goes out the window. All that management science that chewed up a year of your MBA is irrelevant when you're at work and your environment seems out to get you.

In a complex environment, our biggest leadership challenges aren't about personality or projects. They're about context. Strategic leadership is an arena-driven story – and it's time you played your part.

WHAT IS THE ARENA?

Like Roman battle zones, the arena is about more than challenge (plot) or challengers (character). The arena is about the context. The arena is a setting: a visible, communal place where things happen. It's where action unfolds and interacts with the environment; where the actors are visible to the spectators and affected by their reactions; where there is no right answer – just the best response at the time. In the arena, the space is always contested, and it is the environment, not the actors, that sets the scene. Leading in a world gone mad is the same.

When we think in terms of an arena, our focus shifts. Things become less discrete. We transcend people, organisations and sectors, and instead start to focus on the way networks of things, people and organisations interact.

When we make big decisions that matter, we will *always* face multiple objectives and competing values. In the arena, we make constant trade-offs. We know there's no perfect option, so we're intentional about making strategic choices, balancing the short and long term; internal and external progress; and performance, people and politics.

This isn't a sign of things being wrong or harder – it just is.

WE'RE DOING IT WRONG

The classic leadership development arc goes like this:

- We teach people to be technically proficient.
- We train them to manage people.
- We profile their personalities and hope this somehow leads to self-awareness.
- We pin our hopes on an off-the-shelf programme or MBA that does little more than bolster the CVs of those involved.

It's a good start, but it's not enough. It's not working, either – and we know it. A quick dig into the stats paints a worrying picture. Fewer than half of HR bigwigs are confident they're equipping their workforce for the future. Only a quarter of business leaders are confident their people have the right skills to manage incoming change. One in four! We can see the gap, and we know it's not right, but we're charging forward anyway.

If our job descriptions and workforce strategies are to be believed, strategic skills are the most in-demand leadership capabilities. Ninety-seven per cent of senior leaders claim that strategic capability is the key leadership behaviour for organisational success – but 96 per cent of the *same group* insist that they lack time to build this skill. Yes, you read that correctly. We know what we need to do, yet we feel powerless to do anything about it. We're so busy being busy that we're trapping ourselves in a treadmill of futility, and the relevance of what we *are* good at is falling further and further behind.

According to Forbes, fewer than 10 per cent of leaders exhibit strategic skills. Let that sink in for a moment. Nine out of every 10 people we trust to make important decisions don't know how to do it. Herein lies the problem: what we're teaching is great, but it isn't enough. Keen professionals spend, on average, three years getting a classic MBA, but half of it is out of date before they're done.

We're not spending enough time teaching the stuff that never goes out of fashion: how to think and see things differently and respond strategically to change.

It's time for something different. And I've got a few ideas about how to get there.

(Hint: it's not by getting an MBA.)

PREREADING

Watch your language

The words we use have a profound effect on the way we see the world. We can have ideas that we don't yet have words for, but language is more than an explanatory tool: it's both a clue and a lever.

Even small shifts in vocabulary have the potential to trigger significant mindset and behavioural change. After reading *Atomic Habits* by James Clear, I ran a personal experiment. Clear suggests that shifting from 'I have to' to 'I get to' is a powerful gratitude device that could transform our perspective. I was sceptical but curious. So, I tried it.

Words create worlds.

Jonathan Franzen, *Freedom*

For a week, every time I found myself about to say 'I have to' ('I have to cook dinner', 'I have to pick up the kids', 'I have to be in Sydney that week') I swapped it out for 'I get to'.

'I get to cook dinner' suddenly felt like a privilege. We have the food, skills and resources to create a healthy meal, and I'm home to do it.

'I get to pick up the kids' became a lifestyle indicator. Thanks to a harmonious co-parenting relationship, a reliable car and a flexible schedule, I can prioritise my children inside my workday.

'I get to be in Sydney that week' became a marker of work satisfaction. Oh, my work takes me to interesting places to have meaningful conversations with intriguing people? Amazing!

I was stunned by the difference. It triggered a similar exploration in my leadership work. How could we diagnose different patterns of behaviour and thinking based on the language people used? After months of reviewing survey responses and monitoring the words people used in workshops and learning sessions, some clear themes emerged.

The same phrases popped up everywhere, indicating how people approached change and complexity. Worried leaders who used passive language struggled to act on the things they cared about. Busy leaders who spoke in terms of constraints often found it hard to set clear priorities.

When we started to nudge language in a different direction, we saw a corresponding shift in mindset. Channelling the attention of a constraint-focused leader towards the areas they *could* influence, for instance, changed how they approached problems and made decisions.

Most leadership assessments are either insufferably complicated or totally reductive; neither are helpful. Putting the formal tools aside, we learned to map the development and strategic maturity of the leaders we work with, simply by listening. The way people speak and the language they use is so rich with insight that we can pinpoint strategic maturity, leadership maturity and readiness for change within minutes. While leaders stuck in the past tend to be passive in their phrasing, leaders who are focused on the future are more proactive and adaptive.

The ladder on the opposite page shows the link between language, leadership and change. Use it to understand where you, or your peers, are currently at.

WHEN YOU ARE...	YOU SAY	YOU GET	FOCUS ON
ADAPTIVE	*'I'm learning to...'*	Impact	Influence
PROACTIVE	*'I choose to...'*	Focus	Performance
REACTIVE	*'I have to...'*	Action	Systems
PASSIVE	*'I can't...'*	Inertia	Decisions
RESISTANT	*'I won't...'*	Fear	Flexibility

Let's take a look at the different leadership types.

RESISTANT LEADERSHIP

Sounds like: 'I won't'

The fear of change is evolutionary in humans. Since time immemorial, we've always liked routine – and rightly so. Living in certainty has kept us safe. Resistance to change isn't a defect; it's a sensible and necessary response to a world out to get us, where change meant danger. But like many evolutionary responses, it's no longer serving us. If we're fearful of what's coming next and resist change, we can find ourselves frozen in place.

To overcome resistance, learn to cope with change.

To lead through complexity, we need to be OK with change, and that requires **flexibility**. We'll examine this in Module One. Flexible leaders have range. They're in tune with their environment and understand that while it's not all about them, they need to take responsibility. They seize agency, knowing that strategic leadership isn't about getting shit done *despite* your environment, but getting it done *because of* your environment. They recognise that the more senior you are, the more complex and challenging things are likely to be. Flexible leaders get out of their heads because they know it's not enough to think about change – they have to *do* something. They're willing to get it wrong some of the time because they know that's the only way forward. Above all, flexible leaders recognise they need to shift when everything else does – to bend without breaking.

PASSIVE LEADERSHIP

Sounds like: 'I can't'

The fear of mistakes starts from an early age. Well-meaning parents do what they can to prevent kids from making the wrong choices – and this sets a dangerous precedent. Rushing to correct behaviour robs children of an important lesson: that mistakes are experiences to learn from. Worse, it sends a powerfully damaging message: 'we doubt your ability to cope'.

The same patterns play out in the workplace. While 'failing fast' might be the new mantra, we say one thing and do another. Leaders who are afraid of doing the wrong thing don't want to fail. They want to control their environment, and they struggle when they can't. At their worst, passive leaders are perfectionists, never quite confident enough to pull the trigger. When they do, they hedge, relitigate and backtrack.

The most difficult thing is the decision to act,
the rest is merely tenacity.

Amelia Earhart

For passive leaders, the motivation to improve is there, but is often confined to the ideas stage. Meetings are talk-fests, dedicated to all the things that are going wrong, but change is thin on the ground because we're too afraid to take charge.

In Module Two, we'll look at how you can become more confident with change and potential failure by making good **decisions.** Making decisions that stick is a learned skill. When too much time goes into planning, discussing or looking for approval, we think ourselves into a corner. But when we're confident in our ability to find direction, we move towards action. Decisive leaders know that it's not *what* they think but *how* they think that matters. They know that while there might not be a 'right' answer, without space for thinking, we can't take confident action. Decisive leaders provide direction for themselves and their teams that puts passivity behind.

To overcome passivity, learn to set direction.

REACTIVE LEADERSHIP

Sounds like: 'I have to'

The fear of falling behind can make us reactive. The reactive leader has no problem with action. They're busy, stressed and earnest, but all that activity masks doubt about how to make the important stuff happen. I work with a lot of good people and teams who are stuck here and can't break free. Reactive leaders get trapped in a vicious cycle, always looking one step ahead. Everything feels urgent, details take precedence and there's no time for vision.

While being reactive gets a bad rap, it's not all bad – at least you're in motion! We all need to spend some time being reactive, especially in a crisis. Stay here for too long, though, and you'll hit the ceiling. A reactive approach is great for getting things going, but over time it will alienate and exhaust people.

To overcome reactivity, ask better questions.

Reactive people are driven by feelings, by circumstances, by conditions, by their environment. Proactive people are driven by values – carefully thought about, selected, and internalized values.

Stephen Covey

When we're reactive, we work too many hours, hold our teams back and don't see big shifts coming until it's too late. While it's great to act quickly and be concerned about details, the problems arise when we miss the big picture.

Strategic leaders zoom out and break the reactive cycle by thinking in **systems**. We'll dig into this in Module Three. Systems leaders dismantle comfortable silos because they know that building successful teams, organisations and communities means working out how things fit together. They resist the temptation to settle for what's in front of them and focus on seeing and understanding the messy stuff – context, relationships and dependencies – knowing that to do otherwise sets them up for failure. Systems leaders move past finger-pointing and problem-solving to start pulling levers and dissolving issues before they take hold.

PROACTIVE LEADERSHIP

Sounds like: 'I choose to' (or 'I will')

Proactive leaders are masters at taking responsibility. They plan carefully and overcome constraints that stand in their way. Like everything, this is great – until it isn't, because the shadow side of responsibility is control; the fear of letting go. When we hold on too tightly to our environment and attempt to predict the future, we create a bottleneck for innovation. Without trust and confidence, our teams weaken, and stress levels skyrocket.

If you've made it to this point of leadership, pat yourself on the back! Much of the hard work has been done. However, proactive leaders can be the victims of their own success. Getting stuck here can lead to unintentional stagnation as you try fruitlessly to control and predict all the variables.

To overcome proactivity, learn to lead with purpose.

Letting go of the reins and taking a risk on something meaningful is incredibly freeing, and it's the stuff that real **performance** is made of. Purposeful, high-performance leaders take uncertainty in their stride. They are more resilient and less likely to burn out. They know that 'busy' is bullshit, and that performance comes when we understand how to invest our time, money and attention in the things that matter. Performance leaders know that once we eliminate distraction and insist on delivering value, quality and accountability, we've got nowhere left to hide. In Module Four, we dig into what performance is about.

ADAPTIVE LEADERSHIP

Sounds like: 'I'm learning to' (or 'I'm trying')

Adaptive leaders change course and evolve more quickly than their more traditional counterparts, building a self-propelling resilience that compounds over time. Adaptive leaders are generally a step ahead. They pick up on faint warning signals, see beyond the everyday and are driven to make a genuine difference. But they're not always the most popular.

To move on from adaptive leadership, learn to mobilise others.

I gave serious thought to how to put the flow of this book together. All these skills matter in largely equal doses, but there's a natural arc that makes the most sense. While change starts with you, it can't end there:

- You've got to have the right attitude before you can learn anything new (flexibility).
- You've got to figure out what's going on (decisions) before you can start shifting things around (systems).
- You've got to be able to get shit done, so you can make things happen (performance).

But unless you bring others on the journey, your impact will be limited. Move too quickly and you lose people, which is why strategic leaders need to build their **influence** – so that's what we tackle in Module Five.

Only that which can change can continue:
this is the principle by which infinite players live.

James P Carse

Influential leaders know that political savvy isn't slimy; it's non-negotiable for impact at scale. They know that neglecting their reputation and underestimating the human factor makes it hard for people to believe in them, leaving them frustrated and trapped at the starting block. Taking risks and breaking things is fine – but if you're doing it alone, you'll make more enemies than friends. As our environment continues to shift, it will be the leaders who can bring others with them who sustain.

***

There is a natural flow to this book – but don't let that limit how you engage. You'll be tempted to spend the most time on the things you already agree with or understand, but that's a mistake. It's the parts that make the least sense and feel the least comfortable that will encourage the most growth.

There are five critical leadership skills that will arm you for the arena. These five skills, together, are the basis of strategic leadership, and with a full range there's little you can't face. But you can't waste any more time overdeveloping your strengths. There are no compulsory papers here, so choose your own adventure. If you're great at making decisions, but things never seem to work how they're supposed to, focus your energy on systems. If you can make things happen, but it always feels like a solo journey, spend more time on influence.

Most importantly, don't put down the things that are hard. That's where the most important lessons are.

When you need to...	You need...	Focus on...	Read...
Respond to change	Flexibility	Who you are	Module 1
Set direction	Decisions	How you think	Module 2
Make things work	Systems	What you see	Module 3
Make things happen	Performance	Who you do	Module 4
Mobilise others	Influence	Who you touch	Module 5

What we've learned so far

- We aren't equipping leaders to handle complexity.
- The language we use is a clue and a lever for our strategic leadership maturity.
- There are five critical strategic leadership skills: flexibility, decisions, systems, performance and influence.

Your next step

Notice the language you and your colleagues use and reflect on what that tells you about your current leadership mindset.

MODULE 1

FLEXIBILITY

For when you need to cope with change

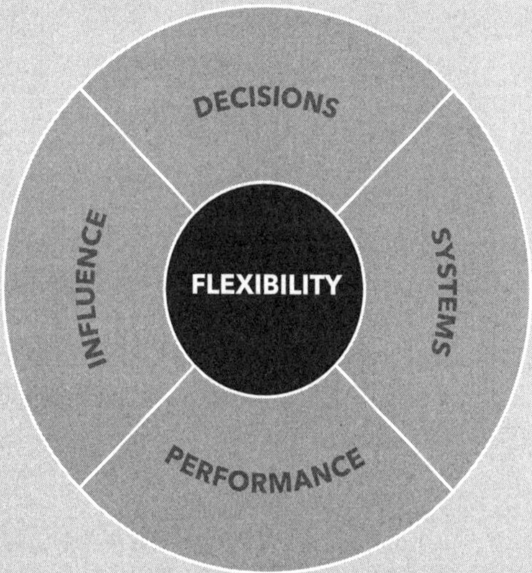

LESSONS IN THIS MODULE

1. Strategic leaders are stretchy
2. You can't work with what you can't see
3. The only thing you control is you
4. Everything's f...raught – and that's fine

LESSON 1

Strategic leaders are stretchy

Things stiffen with time. Even if you're fit and active, your body seizes up with age. By the time you're an adult, your tissues have lost about 15 per cent of their moisture content, making them less supple and more prone to injury. Your muscle fibres start sticking together and tangling up, which is why you get injured when you get old.

Fighting that stiffening isn't easy. Thousands of years ago, people got the exercise they needed by hunting and gathering to survive. In a modern environment, we can sit for days if we're not careful.

We stiffen mentally, too, getting stuck in our ways. We get used to avoiding, escaping or trying to control what we find uncomfortable, and we lose flexibility in how we think and behave. Slowly and insidiously we become trapped, choosing actions based on what we want to avoid instead of what we want to achieve.

As our strengths and abilities propel us forward we double down on them, unintentionally narrowing our range. According to Kaiser and

Overfield, fewer than 20 per cent of leaders qualify as truly 'versatile' as determined by the Leadership Versatility Index. The other 80 per cent are seizing and stiffening over time. Not flash.

Not only do we lack flexibility, we generally don't realise it. Just as we overestimate our IQ, performance and driving skills, we have skewed perceptions of our own capacity for change. Because we think we're stretchier than we are, we tend to blame others for their resistance – unwittingly projecting our own inflexibility.

The good news is: we can do something about it.

To combat modern inactivity, people are turning to yoga. While that's not new – people have been stretching on purpose for more than 5000 years – the last five years have seen a worldwide explosion of yogis. Hundreds of millions of people practise regularly, with converts climbing steadily every year.

The list of purported benefits is long: everything from helping sleep and improving posture to productivity benefits at work. Physically, yoga improves our strength and flexibility. When we intentionally stretch we slow the dehydration process, stimulating the production of tissue lubricants. The lubricants pull our muscle fibres apart and help muscles to rebuild independently of each other.

In psychology, we're stretching too. I recently helped a friend proofread her PhD thesis in clinical psychology. Her research examined acceptance and commitment therapy (ACT), an increasingly popular treatment for everything from addiction to workplace stress. Like yoga, ACT is about stretch – increasing our range so that we can respond to all kinds of situations, especially the uncomfortable ones.

With ACT, we override our emotional instinct to freeze or avoid. For example, we might be anxious about going to work because we know there's a confrontation with our boss on the cards. Our inbuilt response is often to hide – who wants to deal with that kind of conflict if they don't have to? While traditional therapies might *treat* anxiety, ACT supports us to work *with* it. By developing awareness of our surroundings and ourselves and learning to accept things as they are, we stretch our ability to respond when things are hard. Flexible leadership is the same – we can't avoid or control the madness, so we need to work with it.

START AT THE TOP

The test of a first-rate intelligence is the ability to hold two opposed ideas in mind at the same time and still retain the ability to function.

F Scott Fitzgerald

I regularly work with executives who bemoan a lack of innovation and risk-taking in their teams. They can't understand why people are resistant to trying new things and putting themselves out there. It's these exact leaders that are usually the most blind to their own fears and constraints. While the finger often gets pointed at middle managers as a barrier to innovation, the problem usually starts higher up. When asked, only 40 per cent of public managers believed that senior leaders were willing to take risks to support new ideas. Stiffening at the top is unintentionally freezing the middle.

Inflexible leaders don't just make their own lives harder. That lack of stretchiness filters down, stifling innovation and dampening enthusiasm, cooperation and creativity across the board. Without flexible leadership at the top, teams don't cope with change. We're setting people up to fail.

Signs you need to be more flexible

- You're facing change or transition.
- You're feeling stuck or out of your depth.
- Your normal response isn't working anymore.

HIT THINGS WITH YOUR CAR

In my first job out of university I was a policy analyst in local government. Each year, we updated our policies, going through the register to make sure that rules and guidelines were still relevant. Like most small councils we had a lean policy team. With no infrastructure, governance or regulatory policy specialists, we all did a bit of everything – and regularly found ourselves involved in things we'd never be exposed to in a larger organisation.

In one of my first review jobs, I had to go through our infrastructure policies – a hospital pass if I've ever seen one. In provincial councils, engineers are hard to get and battle a workload that well exceeds their capacity, so their tolerance for conversation is slim. Pesky customers, fluffy policy people and annoying accountants aren't appreciated – they've got things to get on and build!

Nervously fronting up to our busy Roads Manager, I worked through his policies as quickly as possible to check that our rules still made sense. This wasn't an easy task – an engineer had written the original policies, which is always a red flag for readability. (I don't know what it is about roads, but we seem to make up words that don't exist anywhere else. Since when was 'roading' a word? It's not a verb!)

Things were going reasonably well until we got to a section on what people could build outside their properties. It read something like:

> *All structures inside the road reserve must be frangible.*

Not wanting to look stupid (but genuinely baffled) I piped up: 'What on earth does "frangible" mean? Do you mean... fragile?' Shot a withering glance, I was quickly corrected.

'Frangible' has since become one of my all-time favourite words. I'm no engineer, so my definition is dicey, but the gist is: for something to be frangible, it (not you) must break if you hit it with your car.

When all structures in a road reserve are frangible, gates, letterboxes and fences will topple over in an accident, rather than standing strong and killing people. Its why rural letterboxes are on wooden poles, and you won't see a brick fence on a freeway or motorway.

Just like our 'roading' (there's that word again) policy, we all need to make sure the right things are frangible. When we decide what we're willing to let break, we make sure that the most important thing – you – is OK.

You might crash into unexpected obstacles occasionally, but when you do, you need to come out all right. I'll grant that the analogy isn't perfect, but if our environment is the road, I think we need to be more the driver than the letterbox. Everything around us might topple over and crash, and we might get a bit dinged up now and then, but when that happens, *we* still need to be OK.

Flexibility means you can bend without breaking. You need to know when it's time to bend and trust that you can. And when things turn to crap, it's critical you can get back up.

Flexibility demands three core skills:

1. *Awareness* – knowing when to bend. You can't work with what you can't see, so we need to understand what's going on inside and around us to respond in more useful ways.

2. *Agency* – trusting that you *can* bend. Most things are outside of your control, so you're the only thing you can change. Awareness might open your eyes, but agency requires you to *do* something.

3. *Resilience* – coming back better. Resilience is not about strength; it's about building your capacity to accept, prepare for and overcome discomfort and failure, because those things are inevitable.

What we've learned so far

- If we don't intentionally stretch, we stiffen with time.
- Inflexible leadership stifles entire organisations.
- We need to be able to bend without breaking to cope with change.

Your next step

Consider the behaviours you're hanging onto that aren't serving you anymore. Could it be time to stretch?

LESSON 2

You can't work with what you can't see

Senior leaders are more likely to overestimate their skills and abilities than the general population. It's not because they're arrogant (well, not always), but because it's hard to stay aware as you move up the ladder. Experience and power make objectivity difficult, because awareness is tricky without good signals. External awareness is hard to come by when you're a leader, because people are less comfortable giving you candid feedback when their jobs and reputations are on the line. Self-awareness gets harder the higher you climb up the ladder, too – when we're highly experienced we have great instincts, so we're less likely to do our homework or question ourselves. When those forces align, it's a perfect storm: we get overconfident about how well we know ourselves, and we misjudge how others view us.

To stay aware, even when the signals are off, we need to do three key things:

1. Understand ourselves, as though we're watching a movie of our own lives

2. Understand our environment, by thinking with others and paying attention
3. Spot opportunities for change, by joining the dots.

WATCH YOUR MOVIE

Flexible leadership is a 'meta competency'. It requires the ability to observe and understand your own thoughts, feelings and situations as though you're not inside them. That kind of awareness requires us to understand two worlds at once: the one inside our heads, and the one outside. This is easier said than done. While most people think they're self-aware, it's a rare quality. Less than 15 per cent of people meet the criteria.

Awareness comes in many flavours. To be a flexible leader, you need two types of awareness: internal and external – and most people are better at one than the other. So, you might understand yourself well but use that knowledge to rationalise your behaviour and misjudge how other people view you. Or you might be attuned to how others perceive you, but have little connection to your inner world and what motivates you to behave the way you do.

There's no shortcut here. The reality is, we don't change unless we understand what's driving our behaviour, or how we got here. When we can spot the patterns that developed and embedded early in our lives and careers – and understand why – we can move past them. We should approach ourselves with curiosity, to ask: why did I react like that? What did I make that mean? Why do I keep making the same mistakes? Once we get what drives us, we can make better decisions and build more satisfying relationships with others.

There's a limit to this navel-gazing, though; a point where introspection becomes negatively correlated with an openness to new information. When we spend too long in our heads, we risk crafting explanations for our behaviour that make logical sense but aren't necessarily true.

So rather than endlessly analysing *why* and getting trapped in an internal loop, we need to shift our attention to *what* we can change about our behaviour to move forward, and how. The Leadership Versatility Index, my favourite 360-degree feedback tool, is great for this: rather than giving you an acronym to work with or listing your traits, it focuses on the specific behaviours you should do more or less of to become a more flexible leader.

You don't need a fancy 360-degree tool to do this, though. When in doubt, *ask someone you trust*. Truth-tellers who care are a powerful advantage. Instead of sitting in a therapist's chair or trying to judge people's facial expressions, just turn up, ask questions and listen. The truly self-aware go out of their way to have uncomfortable, honest conversations with people who know and care about them, so they've got a regular stream of useful feedback about how they behave and how that impacts others.

The most important reason to build our awareness is to make better decisions about how we react. Why bother otherwise? We should learn to observe our behaviour with wry amusement, as though reading about ourselves in a book or watching ourselves in a movie. When we master this perspective, we get out of our heads and into our lives, and we can start to stretch without internal hang-ups holding us back.

Remember: leaders are made, not born. The 'making' is a continuous process that is never finished – and with that attitude, awareness becomes an everyday job. Staying open, understanding yourself, seeking genuine feedback and focusing on the behaviour you can change makes it possible to move forward with perspective and detachment.

Who are your truth-tellers that care? How can you access a stream of useful feedback that will keep you on course?

THINK WITH OTHERS

Have you ever read something aloud and then realised it didn't make sense? Me too. Spare a thought for my children, who've been listening to segments of this book on repeat for weeks! There's a reason why speaking aloud works: building on ideas with others, and having to explain them, makes your thinking deeper and clearer. Its why teaching is the best way to learn. When we think out loud and with others, we use three distinct areas of the brain rather than one, which encourages new neural pathways and connections and helps us to be more reflective and creative. It even makes us better problem-solvers – we make 78 per cent fewer errors when we think out loud than when we silently work through issues in our heads.

Because thoughtful conversations involve more parts of your brain than just reading and writing, they increase your cognitive capacity and help you consolidate new information into memory. The Socratic method is one version of this and one of the most effective ways to stimulate critical thinking. In Plato's dialogues, Socrates asks guiding questions and provides disruptive prompts so his students structure their thoughts better and articulate their learning more clearly. In my weekly *What's on Your Mind?* podcast with Digby Scott, we use this method to test our thinking and get new perspective, poking each other to stretch the boundaries of our ideas. The best leaders and facilitators use these techniques, too, asking tricky questions and posing wild thought experiments to get people thinking creatively and solving problems.

I have some of my best ideas when I'm podcasting with Digby or debating with my friend CV over a glass of wine (caveat: it could be the wine). This isn't just fun – it's social intelligence in action. Social intelligence stretches us by making our ideas more compassionate, relevant and connected. When we become aware of how our ideas are received, we reflect on them more deeply, making them better.

Find a forum where you can experience social intelligence – at work, or with a friend or colleague. Join a community of practice, attend conferences and lectures and talk about your ideas with people regularly.

PAY BETTER ATTENTION

Anyone who's spent time with a four-year-old will remember the incessant questioning stage. Why is the sky blue? Why does that man look like that? Why do we have to do this? Why? Why? Why? It's an exhausting stage for parents (and bystanders!) but critical to the development of a child's mind.

At some point, we lose the habit of questioning. It's hard to stay externally aware, thanks to our lazy brains. We're not good at seeing the difference between what's essential and what's just top of mind. That's not a failing, but more of a wiring issue. We're clouded by cognitive biases that put recency, visibility and familiarity first, making it hard to know whether we're judging our context accurately. It's our brain's way of making things easy for us, driven by what Daniel Kahneman calls System 1 thinking – keeping us efficient with shortcuts to make decisions.

On the daily, System 1 is useful and important. If we had to carefully analyse every choice we made, we'd be worn out by morning tea! But shortcuts can be a problem. When we're working out what to notice and prioritise, shortcuts trip us up – unless we can override them and analyse our behaviour in context. External awareness asks us to hit pause and open our eyes: what's really going on here?

Flexible leaders are impossibly and annoyingly curious. You will often hear them quoting an off-the-wall article they read or starting sentences with 'Isn't it interesting how...' Annoying, maybe, but they're onto something. A curious mindset helps us make fewer mistakes, innovate more, clash less with others and perform better at work. It's good for your career, too. According to the World Economic Forum, curiosity is the factor identified in 30 years of research as the single biggest determinant of professional success.

If you're not naturally curious, don't panic – you can develop it. Before worrying about changing things, you need to start noticing things. Just listening and staying open is most of the job. There's an infinite amount of knowledge and insight out there, and every problem and interaction offers the possibility to learn something new.

Read widely. Ask more questions. Develop an appetite for ideas and build relationships with people who think differently to you. Engage in reflective thinking to examine your choices and those of others. Wonder: why did we do this? What were we trying to achieve? How did others feel about it? How do I know that? What influenced our decisions and actions? What were the consequences of those decisions? Why?

JOIN THE DOTS

My favourite definition of creativity is buried inside a little book called *Mindfulness for Creativity* by Danny Penman. He defines creativity as 'the ability to perceive the world in new ways, to find hidden patterns, to make connections between seemingly unrelated phenomena and to generate solutions'. Not magic, not talent – perception, patterns, connections and solutions. Creativity is all about joining the dots in new ways – finding unseen links and working out what they could create.

When it comes to flexibility, creativity isn't just for the artists, and it isn't just for fun – it's useful, important and takes work. According to the World Economic Forum, creativity is the third most important skill for employees in 2020, behind complex problem-solving and critical thinking. Those skills aren't separate; they're different sides of the same coin. Your job as a flexible leader is to take your creative capacity seriously by making connections and engaging your imagination.

Without finely tuned awareness, you can't see the dots, much less join them. But when you practice asking questions about how things fit together – where they're different, where they're similar and what the opportunities are – your brain starts to fire differently.

Look at examples from different sectors or industries to make new connections. Consider potential versions of the future. Paint them in colour. Build them as a model. Write them down. Say them out loud. Draw a picture of them. Run thought experiments about outlandish scenarios and have crazy ideas.

What we've learned so far

- You can't work with what you can't see.
- Senior leaders find it harder to stay aware because of their status and success.
- You can build awareness by knowing yourself, paying attention and joining the dots.

Your next step

Find a truth-teller who cares, ask them some uncomfortable questions and listen to what they have to say.

LESSON 3

The only thing you control is you

American Beauty is one of my favourite movies. In one memorable scene, we watch Ricky's video of an empty, wrinkled plastic bag tossed about in the wind. We follow the bag as it whips about violently, spiralling skyward then floating to the ground.

Have you ever opened your calendar to find nothing but other people's priorities staring back at you? Look at it now and see.

It happens quickly, and your calendar is just the tip of the iceberg. If you've ever felt swept up in the rhythm or frustrated by the lack of space for stuff you care about, you're not alone. Many well-intentioned people feel a bit like Ricky's plastic bag. Pulled and tugged in all directions, they find themselves at the mercy of other people's choices and priorities.

However, unlike a plastic bag, you have agency. You can't control the wind, but taking responsibility for your actions is the mark of real leadership.

We don't know when the next pandemic will hit. We can't control how our boss shows up today, what the economy will do or whether our customers will be sold on our next big thing. But we do have absolute control over our response – and that agency is what flexible leadership is all about.

As Henry David Thoreau wrote: 'Things do not change; we change'.

We can seize our sense of agency by:

- Living our values
- Having conviction in our thoughts and ideas
- Creating our own rules
- Seeking discomfort
- Making better choices.

STAND FOR SOMETHING

Our values are extensions of ourselves.
They are what define us.

Mark Manson

In 2016, PayPal took a stand that made waves. When CEO Daniel Schulman discovered that North Carolina violated transgender rights by requiring people to use bathrooms corresponding with the gender on their birth certificates, PayPal cancelled construction on a new corporate office in Charlotte. It moved it, along with 400 jobs, to a different state. It was a controversial move, but it aligned with PayPal's purpose to 'focus on what connects us, instead of what separates us'.

PayPal took a stand on diversity early when it decided to forbid websites that promote violence, hatred or intolerance from using its platform. These values have guided the company's business decisions ever since.

The PayPal story shows that being flexible is as much about what *doesn't* change – our values – as what does. Living your values is extraordinarily freeing and simple. The secret thing about values is that when you know them, living by them doesn't make life harder – it makes things easier. When you know what you're not willing to compromise on, you can let go of everything else. When we know and live our values, we're more connected to our behaviour and we can focus on what matters.

Not all our decisions are big curly ones. Most of them are small and cumulative. Every day, we choose how we spend our time, attention and energy – even when it feels as though the control is out of our hands. Every day, those small actions add up to tell a story about what we value most.

So, how do you find your values? I quite like some of the online tests that are out there, though you'll have to give your email address. Otherwise, you might try thinking about what you most detest in others – the reverse is probably a core value for you. If you hate lateness, you value reliability. If stinginess annoys you, you value generosity. If groupthink grinds your gears, you value independence.

For bonus points, try upgrading your first iteration. Not all values are created equally – Mark Manson has a great blog on this. Bad values are uncontrollable and all about how we feel, but good values are things we can control and are more carefully considered. Feelings-based values lead to distorted, short-term decisions, but when we can choose better values, we live a better life – and, ultimately, we can be better people.

As Manson argues, abstraction is useful. So, if you realise you value money, consider whether it might be more about security or freedom. Chasing money can be a trap, but prioritising security or seeking freedom can give you a better life. If you realise you value popularity or crave social validation, consider whether you could value connection instead – or compassion for others. If work or ambition always rises to the top, consider valuing contribution, or perseverance.

When we abstract, we commit to values that lead to better long-term choices, focusing on things we have agency over. You can't always control how much money you have, but you do choose how you spend your time and attention, or which items take priority in a crunch. You can't control whether people like you, but it's up to you how genuine you are and what you do to serve others. You don't know if you'll be promoted, but you can always find a way to contribute, or to overcome obstacles.

Ask yourself: what are your core values? What are you supporting right now, even tacitly, that doesn't align with your values? How would it feel to change those things?

GO AGAINST THE GRAIN

In the 1950s, Solomon Asch ran a series of experiments on groupthink. Participants in groups were asked a series of questions – but they didn't know all of the other participants in the group were actors who'd been coached in advance to select the same incorrect answer, putting pressure on the one participant who wasn't in on the secret. The results were stark. When not exposed to the actors' incorrect answers, people made the right choice almost every time. But when faced with pressure to conform, most caved and 75 per cent answered incorrectly, along with the group.

Nobody wants to be a lone voice in the wilderness; not because we're weak, but because the desire for harmonious groups is a basic human instinct. We evolved to prioritise belonging because, for a long time, it was the only way we could survive. But groupthink is dangerous. Instead, we need conviction in our voice.

Flexible leaders trust in their thoughts, opinions and questions – and that confidence has a flow-on effect. When leaders model permission for dissent it empowers others to speak up too, building a culture of safety and independence. Remember: if you think it, somebody else probably does too, but they haven't had the confidence to speak up. Flexible leadership requires you to take that risk.

(Important note: confidence doesn't mean being a jerk. Flexible leaders are open to being proven wrong. They are just as committed to embracing other opinions, and gracefully acquiescing when needed, as they are to expressing their own views. It goes both ways.)

When have you fallen victim to groupthink? Think about times you wish you'd spoken up: what might have been different?

MAKE YOUR OWN RULES

You take your life in your own hands, and what happens?
A terrible thing: no one to blame.

Erica Jong

Three years ago I cleared Mondays in my calendar, and 'Mummy Mondays' were born. It was radical at the time – my practice had just taken off, and there weren't enough hours in the week. But I knew then that if I didn't carve out quality time with my girls, especially before my youngest started school, urgency would eat away my time until they were left with nothing but scraps.

As it turns out, the world didn't stop. Until Harriet started school, I never worked Mondays, and pretty much everything waited until Tuesday. (Full disclosure: sometimes I did work stupid times on Sunday, Monday and Tuesday nights!) Drawing a line in the sand about my values – quality time with my kids – meant I had to make my own rules, and the rest of my life had to fit.

You might not be able to change the days you work, but everyone has the power to make some rules of their own. True freedom isn't about an *absence* of rules or constraints; it's the power that comes from taking responsibility for your own.

What rules can you create to make your values and priorities a reality?

FIND COMFORT IN DISCOMFORT

In early 2020 I had a group of politicians walk out of a workshop and refuse to come back. It was the first (and may not be the last) time this has happened, and while the reasons were complicated, there was one key issue: I'd challenged some core beliefs about the relationship between elected officials and influential stakeholders, making some of them deeply uncomfortable. When we're uncomfortable, our instinct is to shrink, or retaliate – to avoid what doesn't feel right. It's in that zone of discomfort where real agency lives.

Ask tricky questions. Challenge yourself and others. Think openly – and critically. Critical thinking is an overcomplicated buzzword, but put simply, it's about uncomfortable questions. It's about examining things that don't look like they're up for debate and prodding them to see what they rest on. It's about looking for what isn't being said and testing the validity of what is.

You don't have to start by challenging others, though (they might walk out). To begin, try looking inward and gleefully rebutting your own arguments.

Ask questions that probe, like:

- What's an example of this? What's an example of the opposite?
- What is this really about? How are these things connected?
- Why does this matter? Who does this serve? How does this relate to our goals and direction?
- Is there a different way to explain that?

Asking tricky questions means more than just avoiding discomfort – it means *looking* for ways to be uncomfortable. It's there, in the awkward bit, where the magic happens.

What opportunity to do you have to rebut your own thinking? Try adding a 'rebuttal' section to your reports, emails or business cases. (This book had one for each chapter, in the draft stage!)

DO THINGS DIFFERENTLY

Between stimulus and response, there is a space.
In that space is our power to choose our response.
In our response lies our growth and our freedom.

Viktor Frankl

Like values, reactions based on emotions are problematic. This is why flexible leaders don't react; they respond. They stop to consider what they're trying to achieve before they open their mouth.

When your boss is angry (and wrong) about your project performance, your instinctive reaction might see you defending yourself and fanning the flame, but a considered response would look quite different. If your goal is to keep the project on track, you could instead choose to swallow your pride, appreciate that your boss is engaged in your work and keep things tracking forward. When you let go of your initial emotional response, you can take agency for your results. When you're vulnerable to rapid response (I know a little something about this!) you can shoot yourself in the foot.

Try to choose responses that get you closer to what you're trying to achieve, rather than giving in to a reaction that soothes your neurosis. Before you respond to an email or speak in a meeting, take that split second between stimulus and response to pause. Think first, speak second.

Just knowing you need to change won't make it happen. Identifying 'agile' as a leadership value won't make you more flexible. Putting it on a poster with some SmartArt and sticking it on the back of a toilet door won't do it, either. Identifying what needs to change and becoming aware of the behaviour you're avoiding *without doing anything* is more frustrating and upsetting than pure ignorance. At least when you didn't realise things were a problem, you could be happy!

Ultimately, your life is a series of choices. Every day, in every interaction, you get the opportunity to pick your attitude and response. When we take responsibility for that response, we can be intentional with those choices. I like to use my values to create questions: would I be proud to share this story with my children at dinner? If this response was my only appearance in a movie, would I be happy with how I was represented? Your questions will look different depending on your chosen values, but they should be a useful test for your behaviour and responses as you move through the day.

Each of your values and rules should come with proof. Look at your calendar, commitments and relationships and ask: is it obvious what really matters to me? If not, what could I change?

How we spend our days is, of course,
how we spend our lives.

Annie Dillard

Transformation is a long game and rests on a foundation of small, regular practices that align with our goals and values. When we make incremental changes that help us to do better, we become better.

With regular and consistent practise, those habits will take care of your goals by becoming an effortless part of your daily life. We're always going to have bad days, but when we have good habits to fall back on, our progress will be more consistent.

So, if you know you want to eat better, develop the habit of planning your lunches a week in advance. If you know you get frustrated with your team, create the habit of mirroring their words to understand their feelings better. If you know you're too responsive to email and it's taking you away from more important work, put yourself on 'do not disturb' for an hour every day. Make small, sustainable changes to improve your life.

What small new habits could you establish to get you closer to your goals and values?

What we've learned so far

- Agency is a powerful weapon to change the way you perceive and respond to the world around you.
- Excuses are easy, but agency asks you to take responsibility for your choices.
- You can build agency by knowing your values, going against the grain, making your own rules and finding comfort in discomfort.

Your next step

List your most important values. Think about the ways that you aren't living those right now – and how you can change that.

LESSON 4

Everything's f...raught – and that's fine

Few significant catalysts feel good. I don't know why we insist on talking about growth as though it's a positive, feel-good, sunshine-filled event. Growth and regeneration require pain. Think about the hardest and most important decisions you've had to make – breakups, resignations or health issues. How much pain did you absorb before you finally took action?

I once had to leave a toxic relationship. I knew there was no hope, but I didn't leave immediately – even once the worst revelations were out in the open. I agonised over the decision, hanging on for months of misery before I finally pulled the plug. Why stay and suffer in the face of such terrible treatment? Simple, really: we're programmed to cling to the familiar, even when it's hurting us. The threshold for transformation is high.

Experiences like these are awful, but they're important, because we rarely feel pushed to transform when everything is going well.

Growth is born of challenges, changes and breaking points – and that's as true for our organisations and teams as it is for us personally.

In psychology, it is generally accepted that people respond to stressful situations in one of five ways:

1. Resistance
2. Acceptance with suffering
3. Avoidance
4. Acceptance with action
5. Reframing.

In the fifth response, people alter their experience of a situation by changing their perception, examining their underlying assumptions and asking themselves: what if something else was true?

What if this wasn't what I thought? What if it was going to happen anyway? What if this was an opportunity, not a failure? What if I missed something important? What if this wasn't the right job for me? What if I was the one in the wrong? What if this needed to happen for me to grow? What if it's me that needs to change?

Nothing that happens to you is inherently good or bad, it just is. Nietzsche used the Latin phrase *amor fati*, which translates to 'love of one's fate' – to 'not merely bear what is necessary, still less conceal it… but love it'. Radical, eh? We don't just need to *manage* adversity, but to *love* it. To embrace and be grateful for everything that happens to us, whether it looks positive, negative or neutral.

Your frame will determine what things mean – and this is the stuff true resilience is built of: perspective, risk and growth.

NO MORE BACK TO NORMAL

When I was at university, a cash-strapped student and single parent, I spent a lot of time budgeting. Every dollar counted! But it was always based on the ideal situation, and every week, there would be an exception. Have you ever budgeted like that? 'As soon as we get this bill sorted, or move past this unexpected expense, or when things settle down, we can get back to normal.'

After the initial shock wore off with COVID-19, I noticed a similar pattern. People put their projects on hold and delayed decisions until things 'settled down'. But the settle-down gamble is a dangerous game. When we do that, we assume that change, and the need to adapt to it, is a temporary phenomenon; a wee hump to get over before things get back to a safe normal.

A new expense or issue will always pop up to derail the ideal budget. There will *always* be change and uncertainty – whether it happens incrementally or all at once, and whether or not we see it coming.

A person who wants to think outside the box
is better off thinking inside a box.

The Decision Book

Necessity is the mother of invention. When we face constraints, we tend to make better decisions because we engage different parts of the brain.

Resilience is not about coping with change, managing the fallout or eliminating constraints. It's about succeeding *because* of our challenges, rather than despite them. Sure, it would be nice to hit pause when things went crazy so that we could plot the next steps without the distraction of our existing responsibilities. But that's not how life works at the top.

> *'Sorry, I haven't been able to do much on this, with everything the way it's been...'*

You could say that every week if you wanted to. And the more senior you get, the more likely it is that your excuses will delay progress.

Flexible leaders know those excuses aren't good enough. If you're flexible, you can roll with the punches. If not, you'll live in a stop-start world where progress towards the stuff you care about gets further and further away.

Traditional time-management is all about making to-do lists and prioritising and scheduling tasks. If you've got plenty of time with limited interruptions, then go nuts. In those circumstances, your ambitious to-do list with prioritised tasks is a good option.

But if you spend half your time fighting interruptions, distractions and other people's problems, this doesn't work. It just erodes your agency as you play plastic bag with your time and energy. Instead, I like what Parke and Weinhardt call 'contingent planning'. The concept is simple: you plan your day, week or project by thinking about all the stuff that might get in the way, then work out how you'll handle those issues ahead of time.

When we use contingent planning instead of time planning, we get perspective on reality and disrupt its ability to rattle us. When we assume things will go wrong, we aren't thrown so off course when they do.

If you know you have a difficult day, week or conversation ahead, don't leave it to chance. Plan for problems. Take time to consider what might be required. Do your staff need extra support? Is your boss frustrated? You might not avoid the things that throw you off course, but when they happen, you will be ready.

BE WRONG, EVERY DAY

If you're always right, you're doing it wrong. Unless you're doing things that don't work at least 10 per cent of the time, you're stuck and unlikely to be learning. Look, I get it. There's a profoundly human instinct to celebrate our successes and feel ashamed of our failures. But failure is an event, not a characteristic. Failing doesn't make you a failure. If we shift our mindset to embrace opportunities to change, learn and grow, failure is valuable. As a prerequisite for growth, it's necessary.

Nassim Nicholas Taleb talks about *antifragile* systems: those that don't just absorb shocks but become stronger as a result. Take air travel. When a single plane crashes, we take the lessons from that disaster and apply them across the whole industry. Individual failures strengthen the capacity of the entire system, making it safer every time.

As with air travel, antifragility is about improving *because of* failure, building our capacity to manage the next crisis. When we cope with change we build an intangible asset, banking it to draw on for the next disaster. It's a bit like running: every long run that stretches you a bit further creates a new foundation to extend the following week.

Be careful about confusing resilience with strength, though. One of the least understood elements of Taleb's thesis is that for a system to be antifragile, *most of its parts must be fragile*. Evolution is a brilliant example of this. While an individual specimen is exceptionally fragile, the overall system uses life or death as an indicator of success and adjusts accordingly. Your experiences are the same. In plain English: you need to be weak if you want to get strong. When you're vulnerable to pain, you can make sense of your experiences and build new capacity for the future.

Resilience doesn't mean being bulletproof or superhuman; it's just having the willingness to change and shed the bits that don't work by creating opportunities for things to fail.

Look at your last few weeks and ask: am I taking enough risks? What should my failure rate be? Am I encouraging my teams to try things that might not work? How can I do that?

COME BACK BETTER

Three years ago, I found myself sitting for hours in a bookshop in St Kilda, Melbourne, devouring *Supernormal* by Dr Meg Jay. While my kids gave up and headed off in search of cake, I kept turning pages. Dr Jay was explaining why some kids who experience early trauma thrive, while others go on to live a life of misery, analysing a phenomenon known as post-traumatic growth (PTG). Death, loss and disability can break us – but some people, like those in *Supernormal*, truly flourish, gain personal strength, find meaning in their experience and apply lessons that improve their lives.

Like an antifragile system, PTG challenges the conventional idea of resilience, where we aim to bounce back to where we were *before* a crisis. Instead, PTG is about moving beyond where we were before by taking on new beliefs and ideas to support our growth.

While PTG is an ongoing body of work, initial evidence suggests that two key traits predispose someone to transformation after trauma: openness to experience and extraversion. The more open and connected we are, the more likely we are to respond well to disaster. My relationship was a result of that openness, and it was because I'd cultivated that skill that I could reach out to others when things turned south.

When we aren't hung up on how things are supposed to be, and when we make sense with others, we handle stress far better. If we suffer in shame or silence, afraid to admit we've made a mistake, we struggle to see the future or appreciate our resilience. This has enormous implications for leadership and the way we talk about, highlight and cope with tragedy. One of my clients runs a weekly stand-up for her team called 'Fuck Up Fridays', where everyone comes together to share what went wrong that week. By normalising disaster and making sense of it together, the team grows stronger and more open to growth.

Think about the most embarrassing or disruptive event you've managed in the last few years. Do you talk about it with others? Is there a platform for sharing mistakes in your team, organisation or social group? How can you build one?

Let's make something very clear here: failure isn't only valuable when it leads to triumph. Sometimes heroes aren't the ones who overcame the odds, just the ones who failed. Failure isn't a story we should only tell when it has a redemption arc. Sometimes things don't turn out well, and all we get is a lesson. For flexible leaders, that's enough.

What we've learned so far

- Flexible leadership is about awareness, agency and resilience.
- Resilience isn't about getting back to normal; it's about being vulnerable to experience and coming back better.

Your next step

Think about something negative that's happened to you recently and try changing the frame. What could you call that chapter in your life story?

CHEAT SHEET

FLEXIBILITY

What we've learned

Leadership flexibility is about staying attuned to our environment, taking responsibility for our behaviour and learning from our experiences so we can do better next time. By embracing change and following our values, rather than blindly adhering to the unspoken rules of the game, we stretch.

While fixed leaders stiffen with time, losing touch with their surroundings, pointing fingers and trying desperately to control the uncontrollable, flexible leaders do things differently. Accepting that everything's fraught and that's fine, flexible leaders are in tune with what's going on and comfortable with their ability to cope. They take responsibility for their behaviour, knowing it's the only thing they *can* control, and they take a stand where it counts. Always learning and growing, flexible leaders don't avoid discomfort – they recognise failure as a requirement of growth and actively look for opportunities to stretch.

Here are a few attributes of fixed versus flexible leaders:

Fixed leaders	**Flexible leaders**
Lose touch	Attune
Make excuses	Take responsibility
Seek control	Seek learning
Avoid discomfort	Embrace change
Follow rules	Uphold values

What you can do

To be more flexible, you don't need to experience trauma, epiphany or a personality transplant; you just need to practise.

Every interaction, disruption or problem is an opportunity to build your awareness, agency and resilience. Like all muscles, if you don't use it you'll lose it. If you don't keep stretching, you'll stiffen and seize.

Enforce your practice deliberately and consistently, with visible reminders of your thoughts and ideas. One of my mentees puts the key takeaway from each of our sessions on a post-it note on her monitor screen, so she can remember it during the week. Others change their phone backgrounds, set a calendar prompt or stick a picture on the wall. Choose what works for you and commit to continuous improvement.

Legend has it that Benjamin Franklin made a point of focusing on one virtue each week and practising it daily. Cultivating flexibility can be handled in the same way:

- For one week, concentrate on curiosity – read a different article every day and start a conversation with three strangers. When you have ideas, notice them. Write them down. Make them visible and share them with others.
- In another week, try being more confident – speak up in meetings, question decisions that don't make sense or support a lone dissenter.
- The following week, schedule two meetings with people you trust, to get a new perspective on your environment and behaviour.
- Next time you read a report, ask three tricky questions about what might be missing.
- At the end of your next project, practise reflective questioning.
- Next time something negative happens, think of three different interpretations that might be more useful.

CHEAT SHEET

You don't need to do all these things at once, but you should give most of them a go. With consistent practise, your range will start to increase, and you'll stretch the boundaries of your leadership – becoming more flexible and comfortable over time.

Three key questions

1. What's going on here?
2. What do I have the power to change?
3. What can I learn from this?

MODULE 2

DECISIONS

For when you need to set direction

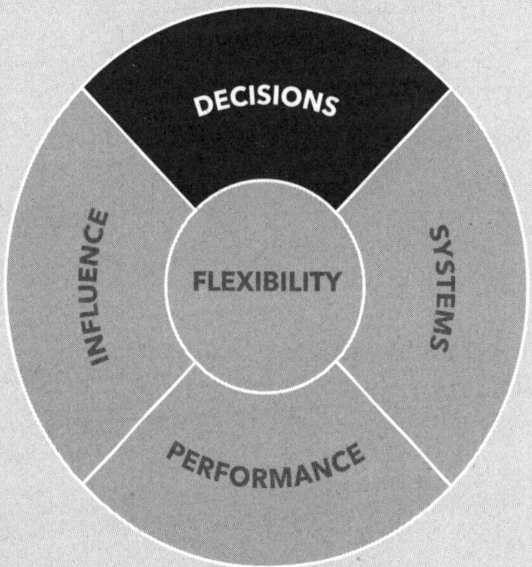

LESSONS IN THIS MODULE

5. Bring thinking back in-house
6. Travel through time
7. Thinking is a team sport
8. Decisions are like babies

LESSON 5

Bring thinking back in-house

I work as a strategist. Large companies and government agencies buy my brain and facilitation skills, to draw out their best thinking and convert it into meaningful direction. What I refuse to do, however, is play the traditional consulting game, with 100-page reports full of fluff and recommendations – because those reports are an accountability cop-out. They're designed so that leaders don't have to make their own decisions.

Somewhere along the line we started to outsource thinking (driven by greedy consulting firms, I reckon).

Strategic thinking is consistently identified as a core leadership capability for senior executives, but strategy skills are taught at less than a quarter of organisations. When I run strategic leadership training, most of the participants tell me it's the first time they've ever been taught how to think.

Strategic thinking is what makes us human. We have the unique ability to go beyond what's in front of us, to notice and store information, to use that to plan for things to be different and to change our behaviour for the future. These skills are our natural competitive advantage – so why don't we nurture them?

LEARN HOW TO THINK

I was a first-generation university student in my family – and my perception of what university would be like was way off. I arrived on campus expecting to see philosophical types in black turtlenecks musing under trees or having engaging coffee-shop conversations about current events. Imagine my disappointment to find a gaggle of grubby teenagers more concerned with their social lives than advancing collective insight.

The most useful thing about university for me wasn't the social opportunities or even the things I learned. I've forgotten most of it. What university did was change my perspective. I realised how many things there were that I had no idea about – and, thanks to a humanities degree, I learned how to think critically about the world around me.

Those skills are enduring, and the reason why – even in a 'future-work' environment full of STEM and micro-learning – long-form, humanities-based education still has incredible value in modern society. The real skill isn't knowing *what* to think – it's knowing *how*.

If the half-life of a skill is down to just five years, imagine what the half-life of knowledge looks like? Assume the value of what you know is expiring as soon as you think it.

Increased decision quality is the single most effective performance intervention for organisations of all sizes. For government, making good decisions can be the difference between making people's lives better, or worse. For business, decision quality is make or break.

Knowing how to think is a sustainable advantage – a muscle you build that makes you sharper, more innovative and ready for change. Military strategists have understood this for centuries. Wars are won in the strategy room, not on the battlefield. Once you're in combat, it's too late to think.

MAKE GOOD DECISIONS

In a recent board workshop I ran with a national sporting trust, I watched a group with more than 150 years of combined experience struggle under cognitive pressure. Their deep understanding of 'how things are done' came up against hard truths about the people they serve. Their solutions were right 20 years ago, but they didn't make sense for a diverse, changing community with less time on their hands and different options for physical activity. Sport might not have changed much, but the people and the environment they were trying to reach had – and they were at a loss to work out what to do next. They knew about sport, but not decision-making.

If we've spent our careers doing our best and getting good results, this might be one of the hardest things to confront. When the problems or their potential solutions are suddenly outside our sphere of knowledge, our instinct is to retreat into details and familiarity. When we don't have an effective way to expose those biases and safely challenge that thinking, our organisations suffer.

Worse, in the public sector, our communities pay the price. We're all battling the pressures of our daily lives, and our time for engagement is slim. We need responsive, relevant public services that see the future *before* we do. If our leaders can't provide us with future-proofed infrastructure, accessible data, pedestrian-friendly transport systems or environmentally sustainable planning rules, our children and grandchildren will bear the cost.

Because we treat decision-making as intuitive, many senior leaders find themselves fumbling around without skilful guidance. As a result, they find themselves operating on a combination of intuition and bureaucracy when it's time to plan for the future.

Signs you need to make better decisions

- You waste time going around in circles.
- Your decisions don't stick.
- Your teams feel uncertain and don't know what to focus on.

Making good decisions is about time travel – learning from the *past*, making choices in the *present* and planning for the *future*. It's about building collective wisdom and treating our choices like babies – always growing, never quite done. Strategic leaders make good decisions that convert uncertainty, which we can't control, into action, which we can – to set direction, lead decision processes and evaluate choices critically. And none of those things can be outsourced. We need to do it in-house.

What we've learned so far

- Strategic leaders know *how* to think, not what to think.
- Improving decision quality transforms organisational performance.
- Poor decisions compromise our future.

Your next step

- Audit your decision-making confidence. Which situations do you find hardest to make a call on?

LESSON 6

Travel through time

Some years ago, I was called to facilitate a strategy session between politicians and senior leaders in a small New Zealand town. There was palpable tension in the room, between the mostly new executive team and long-serving elected councillors. The executive team was brimming with ideas, optimism and plans, but were frustrated by the backwards-looking councillors.

Every time we made progress on investment for the future, a councillor would allude to previous disappointments and project failures, casting a cynical tone over the room. This is common, particularly in organisations that have plenty of 'lifers' – people who've been around the block. It can be extremely frustrating for leaders who just want to get on with it, but it makes sense.

In my workshop, the councillors had been burned by earlier events. They felt misled by a previous chief executive over a landmark project, which suffered overspending and delays. It left them wary of their new leader's advice – even though the blemished project had nothing to do with her.

The past is a foreign country –
they do things differently there.

LP Hartley, *The Go-Between*

It happens in companies, too, where a turnaround leader is brought in to change things up, but the legacy of broken promises, ineffective restructures or bungled change makes people nervous. Even without an adverse history, change efforts butt up against legacy thoughts, patterns and behaviours. For some people, accepting a new way of working can feel like a personal slight, suggesting that the way they've been doing things until now was wrong, which makes *them* wrong. In situations like this, an inability to learn from the past severely hamstrings our capacity to cope with a changing present, much less create a new future.

I see two common decision-making behaviours when it comes to learning from the past:

1. *Dismissal.* Here, changemakers seek to dismiss the past and focus only on the future. While this may work temporarily, dismissal ultimately compounds the impact of failures, destroys the learning opportunity and breeds resentment.
2. *Rumination.* In contrast, we might ruminate – exactly where the councillors were in the story above. Here, we constantly re-live and re-experience the past and its associated feelings. We dwell on the negative, romanticise the positive and close ourselves off to new ideas. This is a dangerous place and can be extremely toxic.

The solution to both is reflective thinking.

Reflection is open and constructive. It focuses on opportunities for learning and identifies areas to change. Reflection honours the experiences and feelings of those who were involved in the journey, and creates a narrative that ties it into future planning. When called in to lead a strategic refresh or reset, reflection is where I'll often start – and was precisely the strategy I used to successfully overcome the tense councillor/executive team strategy session.

Trying to move on in this kind of environment without acknowledging history is a mistake. In my workshop, we used a simple timeline exercise to map our journey over the last decade or so, to recognise the successes, failures, changes and events that had led to our current point. Together, we created a shared narrative that honoured the past, anchored the present and paved the way for talking about the future.

Skilful reflective questions are more specific than 'what did we learn?' and should include things like:

- How did we get here?
- What were we trying to do?
- What challenges did we face?
- Who did we help?
- What's better now, because of what we've done?
- What weaknesses did this expose?
- What was the single most important lesson we learned?
- How can we use our experience to do things differently in the future?
- What would we do if we faced the same problem again?
- Now what? (My personal favourite.)

Build time and space for reflection into your projects, programmes and regular planning days. Resolve to ask useful questions, so that no achievement or failure is squandered.

BE CAREFUL WITH HISTORY

In a classic metaphor, Nassim Nicholas Taleb describes 1000 days in the life of the Thanksgiving turkey. He asks us to consider a turkey that is fed every day. 'Every single feeding', he writes, 'will firm up the bird's belief that it is the general rule of life to be fed every day by friendly members of the human race "looking out for its best interests", as a politician would say'. However, on the afternoon of the Wednesday before Thanksgiving, something unexpected will happen to the turkey: 'It will incur a revision of belief'.

Risk hides. As evidence accumulates to support a particular idea, and people become more certain of its accuracy, we become increasingly unaware of what's coming next. The turkey felt safest right when it was most in danger.

We should be careful with history. The past is an important source of data and information. Evidence-based decision-making is critical to combat bias, prove that our issues and concerns exist and understand causes and effects. Despite that, we need to be careful about how much weight we give to statistics, data and case studies. Where uncertainty is concerned, empirical knowledge has inherent limitations. The more complex our decisions, and the more potential unknowns are involved, the less reliable it becomes. So, in a complex, changing environment, we need to be just as good at turning a *lack of knowledge* into decisions.

To avoid being a turkey, we need to focus on two important things when we're working with information: *meaning* and *completeness*.

When we review quantitative data, for example, we should interrogate the numbers to understand relationships, trends and early warning signs. In New York City, domestic violence reports decreased by almost 40 per cent during the COVID-19 lockdown, suggesting more people were safer in their homes. As a headline figure, this was great, but a more critical interpretation painted a different picture.

Calls to women's shelters had increased sharply during the same period, leaving officials wondering about the disconnect.

Digging deeper, officials understood the situation more clearly. Physical distancing measures to prevent the spread of coronavirus had closed, or limited access to, physical spaces that families often sought help from, or where the system picked them up. Without kids in school, social workers weren't spotting warning signs. With local non-profits working from home, offices were closed, and help centres less accessible. Worse, because people were afraid of contracting the virus, they were more reluctant to enter shelters. Domestic violence wasn't down – the number of people getting help was.

If New York public officials hadn't looked more closely, the consequences could have been disastrous, affecting decisions about funding and support for domestic violence services and exacerbating the situation further. Meaning matters.

We need to ask tricky questions about what we're *not* seeing. Always use logic and intuition to guide the way you review information and work out how believable it is, how reasonable it is and how applicable it is to your current situation.

Things make less sense than we think. Our brains are driven to try to make sense of things, crafting compelling stories that draw everything neatly together. Reality is generally much messier. Resist the temptation to dot the i's and cross the t's when facing contradictions and paradox. If it seems simple or obvious but your problem is complex, you are probably missing something, or reducing the truth.

When reading a report, ask questions like: why did they choose this frame? What question are they trying to answer? What is their intention? Is this true? What assumptions have been made here? Does this make sense? What would it mean if I agreed with this? What viewpoint is missing? What information has been left out? Who gains from this? Whose interests are being served? What counter-arguments are there? Perhaps most importantly: what are the inconsistencies?

History matters… to a point. When it comes to making decisions, the past is both critical and irrelevant. We need time to reflect and learn, gather data, debrief on successes and failures and honour the journey travelled. However, we need to remember that the past can only ever tell us what's already happened. The tools we used to solve yesterday's problems are unlikely to equip us for tomorrow, but they can teach us important lessons about ourselves and our environment. Real strategic insight requires the right combination of reflection and information, with a healthy dose of perspective.

MAKE CHOICES IN THE PRESENT

To finish this book, I holed up in an adorable little cottage in Martinborough. I'd been writing for months, but working in the cracks only got me so far. For the final push, I needed genuine presence: uninterrupted time, a change in location and the headspace that comes with that.

Constant distractions pull at our attention – calls, texts, social media updates, emails, pressures from work, managing our families, news. Its why strategic offsites are so popular. Big-picture thinking requires space to kick off insight and perspective.

> *It's only by concentrating, sticking to the question, being patient, letting all the parts of my mind come into play, that I arrive at an original idea. By giving my brain a chance to make associations, draw connections, take me by surprise.*
>
> William Deresiewicz

The lightbulb moments that change the way you think about a problem can't be manufactured, but they can be nurtured with the right conditions. For me, that's often travel – I have my best ideas on a plane. JK Rowling is said to have drafted the first Harry Potter book on a four-hour train ride.

Thinking rarely happens by accident. There will always be something next on our to-do list, but space requires commitment and discipline. The most successful strategic leaders in the world know this and make the space for it. When Michael Porter followed 27 CEOs of billion-dollar companies for 13 weeks, he found that the average CEO spends 43 per cent of their time on activities that furthered their business. They also spend about 25 minutes every morning strategising and planning, before tackling calls, emails and other operational tasks.

If CEOs of billion-dollar companies can do this, we can, too – but it might look a bit different. Research suggests that if you can achieve the 90/10 rule – 10 per cent of time spent in strategic thought – then you will achieve massive benefits. That's a half-day per week, two days per month or a week per quarter.

How and where can you make the time to be present and think?

YOUR BRAIN IS AN ASSHOLE

The human brain is the most incredible and astounding piece of technology found on the planet and is yet to be replicated. Despite that, we can't trust it.

We make most of our choices through bias, assumptions and heuristics. We get tired and overwhelmed and make silly mistakes. We forget things. We get too tangled in our thoughts to think clearly. None of this makes us terrible – it makes us human. Eckhart Tolle says that when we can't make up our minds, it's *because* of our minds. And thanks to our minds, we come up against powerful biases that affect the way we see things:

- *We're triggered by loss.* When it looks like we might lose something, we get fearful and negative, which compromises our ability to understand risk.

- *We like things we understand.* We naturally gravitate to ideas and solutions we already understand – giving insufficient attention to things we don't, making it difficult to innovate.
- *We get stuck on ideas.* The first idea, number or statistic we hear can become the basis against which other things are measured. This makes it hard to stay open to possibility or evaluate things.
- *We like things to make sense.* The brain favours neat and tidy stories. That means leaving out important pieces of information that might contradict our narrative and skew our memory.
- *We justify our decisions to feel better.* Once something is decided, we look for reasons why we were right, and avoid anything that indicates we weren't.
- *We're swayed by the crowd.* We take popularity as social proof of correctness – even when logic would suggest it's the wrong move.

Together, those biases make our ability to think highly flawed. And when we're tired, that gets worse. I often work with leaders with chronic decision fatigue. Stressed and overwhelmed, they get unexplained headaches, snap at others and make impulse choices. Sometimes they feel incapable of making decisions at all.

This is normal, particularly when our environment is so fast and uncertain. Mental energy is finite. When we need to conserve energy, willpower and self-regulation are the first things that switch off. This is when we're most likely to default to our biases. Overcoming that fatigue needs real intention about how we manage our decisions.

When it comes to memory and easy, repeated decisions, the answer is simple: write everything down, and automate as many decisions as possible by making them ahead of time. Putting thoughts to paper clears your mind and helps you prepare and organise ideas.

We need to make commitments, not decisions, to make life easier for our future selves. Decide as many things as you can ahead of time, put them in your calendar or give them to someone else to manage, and move on.

Above all, accept that your brain is an asshole, and work with it. That way, you have enough space to become aware of some of those other biases and shortcuts. Then you can start asking more challenging questions about how you're making choices – or are you just avoiding loss? Remember your newfound flexibility and remain curious.

How can you give your brain a chance? What commitments can you make now that will give you the space to think clearly in the future?

GO BACK TO THE FUTURE

Bad strategy is the single most common reason for business failure. We just aren't good at it. We tend to have some combination of an in-depth business plan and a high-level vision floating around the office, but genuine strategic direction is less common. Worse, we use all kinds of ridiculous jargon that makes it out of reach to most people.

Strategy is not complicated; it's just poorly understood.

At its essence, strategy is the way we choose to achieve our goals. It's about method ('the way'), choices ('we choose') and outcomes ('our goals'). And it matters, a lot.

Without a clear strategy, we don't have the direction necessary to guide our decisions, we struggle to align people and resources and we don't have a cause to engage people in. Worse, we don't make the best use of time and money, and we're unprepared for change.

The figure overleaf shows the three key components to strategy.

Strategy 101

WHY	Aspiration Long-term Includes: vision, mission, purpose
HOW	Direction Medium-term Includes: priorities, focus, objectives
WHAT	Operation Short-term Includes: plans, budgets, actions

First is the **why**, which captures purpose, vision and mission. These are our aspirational long-term outcomes: the differences that we want to make in the world. When we're clear on that, we can start to make choices about the path we'll take to get there. The *why* level should change very rarely.

Lastly is **what**, which is all about doing: plans, actions and initiatives. It's the decisions you make every day to achieve your goals. The *what* level changes daily, as it should.

In the middle, though, is **how**, which is about the way you work, spend energy and direct focus. The *how* is the guts of strategy. While the *why* is aspirational and long-term, the *how* is intentional and medium-term. The *how* level changes sometimes, but rarely by accident. We should review our *how* regularly, or in response to a significant change.

Most organisations and leaders are relatively comfortable with the *why* and the *what*. We understand our purpose, and we're overflowing with fantastic work programmes and initiatives.

But things get more complicated with the *how*. This is the essence of strategy: the missing middle, the connecting piece that brings together our aspirations and operations.

Done well, it becomes a filter for action and decisions. Good strategy is as much about what you choose *not* to do as what you do. The *how* involves trade-offs about how we allocate resources and attention, which inevitably require us to let people down and put a stop to things already in train. And that's hard to do.

LESS PLANNING, MORE STRATEGY

Most strategic plans are light on the strategy and heavy on the plan – because this is where most managers and many board members feel comfortable. Armed with good intentions, most strategic planning conversations sit somewhere between theoretical navel-gazing and detail-focused talkfests aimed at eliminating the unknown.

This is a terrible use of time and a lost opportunity. Strategic direction that is designed for change and uncertainty should hit the sweet spot: something you can imagine that makes you feel a bit uncomfortable. You're not trying to eliminate the unknowns; you're trying to prepare for a future that's full of them, as best you can, by building your capacity to respond.

A strategic plan is not about *prediction,* it's about *response* – what principles and priorities we can use to guide our future decision-making. It's where we decide *how* to decide when everything changes – which it will!

Rather than defaulting straight to plans and budgets with little or no rationale, a good strategic plan answers these questions with principles or decision rules that create a useful, living reference that we can uphold as our environment continues to change.

Good strategic plans provide enough detail for *direction*, which is useful and empowering, without going so far as to provide a *prescription*, which hamstrings innovation and prevents people from doing their jobs.

For your next strategic plan, think about the questions you're trying to answer, and steer the conversation away from the *what* towards the *how*. Your strategic plan should answer four key questions:

1. Why do we exist?
2. Where are we now?
3. Where do we want to be?
4. How will we get there?

Dig a layer deeper and it should also provide answers to other critical strategic questions, such as:

- What makes us unique?
- What are our operating principles?
- What does success look like?
- How will we measure that?
- What are our top priorities – and why?
- What will we change or stop doing to commit to those priorities?
- What capability will we need to develop to make this a reality?
- How will we respond to new problems or opportunities?

What we've learned so far

- Good decisions require us to travel through time.
- We need to learn from the past – but be careful with history.
- We need to make choices in the present – and that needs space.
- We need to plan for the future – by focusing on how we will get there, even when things don't go to plan.

Your next step

Review your most recent strategic plan against the four key questions. Does it answer them all? If not, what's missing?

LESSON 7

Thinking is a team sport

When COVID-19 hit, many of us experienced financial uncertainty. Businesses lost revenue, people lost jobs and the economy went into a tailspin. Those of us who are self-employed had some serious decisions to make about the way our businesses would manage in a new and uncertain environment.

After a family meeting to work out how to get through lockdown, we made some important financial decisions. How long could we operate without revenue if we lost our existing clients and projects? Was our financial buffer strong enough to continue running our household? What should we do about investments and savings?

We had tough calls to make, including a decision about some money tied up in a market index fund. It was a significant proportion of our reserves and might have been the tipping point for the survival of our household and business if we experienced months of disruption. It was a tricky bind. Index funds are a long-term investment. Successful long-range returns require the confidence to leave the shares alone, even in a dip, to fully realise the investment strategy. But we'd had a big external shock, which needed us to revisit that strategy. Should we liquidate the shares, which had already fallen in value by close to 30 per cent, or take the risk and ride it out?

Ultimately, we chose to liquidate the investment, at a cost. While we couldn't predict what might happen in the market, losing access to the money would be serious, and our need for cashflow, in an uncertain credit environment, outweighed the long-range benefits of holding onto the shares. Taking the hit, we transferred the money, and within weeks, it was clear that our business would continue to thrive, and that the market would recover.

Does that mean we made a poor decision? Absolutely not. Irrespective of the outcome – which couldn't be predicted – our process was sound. We considered our context, weighed up risk, uncertainty and impact, applied clear criteria to our choices, considered our options and committed to a direction. And we made our decision together. The quality of the decision was not about the outcome – it was about the process. And on that front, the decision passed the test.

When it comes to decision-making, knowing how to think and what good decisions look like isn't enough. Contrary to popular wisdom, **what makes a decision good or bad is not the outcome – it's the process used to make it**. While good decisions do not guarantee good outcomes (as in my investment dilemma), consistently good choices do tend to lead to consistently better outcomes.

Decision-making is not a tick-box exercise. Good decisions require us to make space, plant seeds, argue with ourselves and each other and stumble our way around in the dark. It's messy, uncomfortable and annoying.

While we *think* we make decisions in a logical, linear way, the reality is more complicated. The following diagram offers a more accurate version of how decisions are made in the real world.

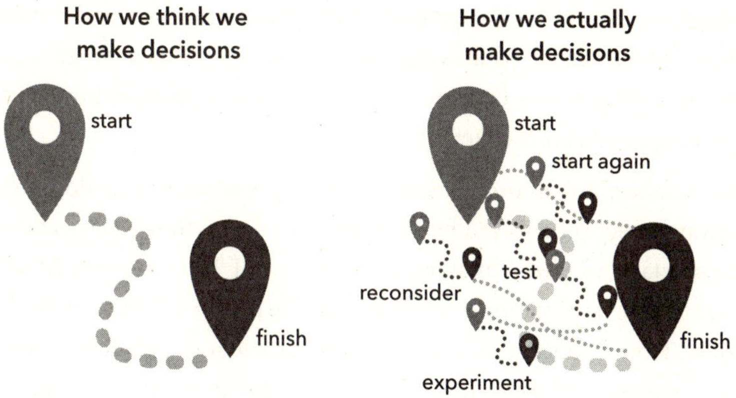

The kinds of decisions you want to make – ones that set new and exciting directions, make bold and brave choices and develop interesting and innovative solutions – don't come from streamlined, linear processes, and they rarely happen if you're making them alone.

Decision processes are rarely straightforward, yet we often design them to be. Jumping back and forth is not a sign that your decision process is failing; it's a sign that you're engaging meaningfully in each stage.

Entering a decision-making process expecting it to be messy – and making that clear at the outset – is an honest and respectful way to work. Most decision processes turn out like that anyway, and when expectations aren't set at the start, people feel unnecessarily frustrated or let down when things don't go smoothly.

The good news is that making decisions together, while not linear or easy, is relatively simple. You need to set a clear **frame**, create a safe and productive **space** and then commit to a **decision**.

SET THE FRAME – WHAT'S THIS ABOUT?

Setting the right frame is all about cultivating awareness: we can't work with what we can't see. We need to understand our context deeply and have a clear picture of the trends, changes and forces that are relevant to what we're trying to achieve. When we get our frame right early, we do a much better job of generating options and making good choices later.

Remember: not all problems need solving, and those that do don't always need to be solved by us. Before we do anything, we need to understand why we're making a decision at all. What's changed that created the need for us to act? What are the drivers behind our decision? How important is it to solve this problem or respond to this opportunity, and what will happen if we don't? What information supports our feelings?

We ask these questions because it's easy to get tunnel vision when we're making decisions. Daniel Kahneman calls this WYSIATI – 'what you see is all there is'. Big-picture thinking requires us to zoom out and appreciate the broader context, asking questions like:

- What's going on, internally and externally, that we haven't thought about?
- What other forces are at play?
- Is there more to this than we've considered?

When you have a handle on the context, it's vital to sort the information for relevance. What is the impact of each of these changes? How much influence do we have over the outcome? Once we have the full picture, we need to focus our energy on only the things that will have a significant impact, and that we have the power to do something about.

Schedule regular sessions with your team (or just yourself) to zoom out. Scan your environment by asking what's going on out there, and internally, and what that might mean for your approach.

It is the mark of an educated mind to be able to entertain a thought without accepting it.

Unknown

Walk a mile

It's hard to get out of our heads. Even when we're trying to stay open, we tend to default to inbuilt mental models for seeing the world. When framing a decision, we need to consider how other people might think.

Practise shifting into others' views and perspectives. When you can do this, you become less attached to your point of view, and you see things from a new angle. Taking on another perspective enhances your socio-cognitive intelligence, which means the more you do it, the better you get at understanding how people think. In an incredible piece of research on awareness and theory of mind, perspective exercises were found so effective that, if practised consistently, they can change your brain structure. Your brain adapts, building social intelligence through neuroplasticity, boosting the ongoing likelihood that you can make decisions that benefit others.

Try playing a game, like one I use in workshops, called 'Fresh Perspective'. By choosing a new identity and stepping into another person's shoes to ask what they say, think, do and feel, you unlock new perspective on old issues and build empathy.

When choosing your frame, consider:

- What information do you have?
- What are your ideas and assumptions?
- What are the gaps?
- What other ideas should be explored?

CREATE A SAFE SPACE – HOW WILL WE MAKE THIS DECISION?

How well our decision-making process works is generally determined by the decisions made at the outset. These include:

- *Who* will be involved – and what role they will play?

- *When* we need to decide – the timeframe and endpoint.
- *How* we will decide – the ground rules for participation.
- *What* a good decision looks like – clear decision criteria.

Who

Ah, diversity. Diversity of viewpoint is enough for a room of old white dudes to get it right… right? Wrong. Real diversity of viewpoint requires diversity of place, space, person and context. It means considering race, culture, gender, age, location, class, position, function and form. It means talking to people who violently disagree with you, those who come from a different place than you and who speak in ways that make you uncomfortable. It means testing your thinking with the people who you don't really want to hear from – the cynics, naysayers, pragmatists and pessimists.

Diversity is also about the way we think. When looking at the ways different people make decisions, try to engage as many of the following five key typologies as possible:

1. *The Protector* is your classic conservative. They protect the status quo with gusto. They're often heard saying things like 'if it ain't broke, don't fix it'. Valuing stability, these people tend to be practical, conservative about risk and nervous about the potential for loss. Testing your thinking with a Protector is a good feasibility check.
2. *The Thinker* moves slowly but carefully. They're rational, they value detail and they are often heard saying things like 'let's not go so fast'. Contemplative and cautious, the thinker seeks good information and spends time weighing potential options. Testing your ideas with a Thinker means you won't miss something important.
3. *The Driver* is all about momentum. Strategic, results-driven and comfortable with change, they value speed over accuracy

and are often frustrated by decision-making processes, preferring to keep things moving. Many current and aspiring chief executives fall into this category, and making sure they're involved is useful to stop getting bogged down in detail.

4. *The Innovator* likes to dream big. Enthusiastic and creative, the Innovator has a vision and is often tapped into emerging signs, risks and trends. Unshackled by the fear and practicality of the Protector, the Innovator struggles with optimism bias and a short attention span but adds incredible value to the generative parts of any discussion.
5. *The Mediator* is focused on people. Compassionate and sensitive, the Mediator seeks to compromise and will be the tempering force in a tough decision. Generally heard asking 'how can we make this a win-win?' the mediator protects relationships, negotiates risk and is a gem in business change planning with people implications.

Think about the people you need involved in your next decision-making process - do you have all your bases covered? Who else might you need to include?

Be careful about how you frame people's input. I've watched this done poorly, particularly in the public sector. When people dedicate their time and energy to a strategy process, they will feel disappointed and disengaged when they don't get a say in the final choice, or the decision doesn't reflect their thinking. Making decision rights clear at the beginning will prevent this from happening. Not everyone needs to be involved with the full process, and not everyone gets a say in the outcome – but they do need to know where they fit. People don't mind having low stakes in a decision – they just need to be made clear about what will happen with their input, and have their feedback valued and acknowledged.

For your next decision, try mapping the roles and responsibilities of each person. Challenge yourself by asking who is really needed for which stage and be sure to communicate clearly with each person ahead of time.

When

Some decisions seem to drag on forever. Ironically, they are usually the decisions that present with an initial sense of urgency but wind up in endless bouts of relitigation and confusion. While putting a timeframe around solving complex challenges can feel like asking the length of a piece of string, trying to make decisions without clear milestones and a defined endpoint is a mistake.

Right-sizing time is imprecise – strategic decisions can take anywhere from days to years, and there is no exact science to getting it right. Like Parkinson's Law: work will expand to fill the time available for its completion.

What you can do, however, is set a deadline, and make the critical checkpoints clear. The deadline can be renegotiated as necessary, but it at least gives people something to work towards. With no end in sight, motivation drops away, and the likelihood of getting to action quickly reduces. You need to book the time to make them happen – making decisions faster requires consciously creating the time to make them.

While important decisions should generally have a long-term horizon, commit to making the smallest possible decision and moving on it quickly. Generally, the best way to learn is to take action – this provides opportunities to refine your thinking early.

For your next decision, set a deadline for your first experiment. Ask yourself what the smallest possible decision you can make is and aim for that.

How

When talking about curly issues like, say, environmental sustainability, we often collide with our participants' political positions or personal belief systems. While a political debate serves no-one, making these decisions based on cold hard facts is rarely the answer, either. We need to get the right balance between ideas and identities if we want to engage our group in thinking about the long-term impact of our choices, build commitment to our chosen path and land on a direction that's meaningful to our context.

While identities are about what we *believe* to be true, ideas are about what *might* be true. Getting stuck in either camp holds back progress. When we're tangled up in what we believe to be true, personal issues and agendas creep in, clouding our judgement. When change is mooted or orders are challenged and people take it personally, this stops the conversation or decisions from moving forward.

However, when we try to separate identity from ideas and think of ourselves as completely objective or impartial, we lose the worth of lived experience and values; we bury hidden bias and lose meaningful connection. The trick is to find the space in the middle – to move from ideology to purpose, and from beliefs to values. By finding the common thread in even the most opposing position, you make it safe for people to align without compromising the things about themselves they hold close.

Next time you're in a challenging conversation, try finding the thread in people's thinking – this is usually about values or big-picture goals. Steer the conversation there to find a new way forward.

What

When you're excited about an opportunity or battling with a significant challenge, it's tempting to jump straight to the ideas phase. It's often where we start – people come in with a bright idea, and they want to get moving on working out the details.

This is great! It means we're invested in the process and committed to finding a solution. But if we go straight there without taking the time to nail out criteria, we can launch into answers that don't solve our problem.

At this stage of the process, take the space to confirm what a good decision looks like, by asking:

- What are the most important outcomes we need to deliver?
- What weight would we ascribe to each of these outcomes?
- How will we test alignment with our big picture?
- How important are cost and feasibility?

Only once you're clear on how a decision will be assessed should you continue to the next stage.

MAKE A DECISION – WHAT ARE WE GOING TO DO?

This bit tends to be treated like a black box – stuff goes in, stuff comes out, and who knows what happens in between. But by ideating, arguing and poking holes, we can make decisions that matter.

Our first idea is rarely our best one, and the most creative innovations in history took countless attempts to get right. It took Sir James Dyson 5126 design attempts before he got a properly working vacuum, hundreds of prototypes before the Wright brothers got a plane off the ground and over 1000 unsuccessful attempts before Thomas Edison created the first lightbulb. Don't give up too early.

There's no shortcut to this bit, and nor should there be. The process of ideation and testing should be thorough, enjoyable and iterative.

In your next decision-making process, try using cheeky questions to provoke thought experiments. What if you only had half the time or half the money? What if you had 10 times as much time or money? What if you had to do something fun? What if you didn't have to answer to anyone? What's the worst idea you can think of? Use those ideas to test the bounds of your thinking.

We should use the decision criteria we established in in the last step (our most important outcomes) to evaluate the suitability of our ideas, systematically working through our options and assessing them. For complicated decision processes, this might require a full business case and economic analysis. For smaller decisions, this might be based on individual or collective gut feel. For things in the middle, a simple matrix will often do the job.

Regardless of how you do it, the key players in a decision should gather to decide how each option stacks up and provide the rationale behind their thinking. Take heed, though: if this feels clear-cut, it could be a problem. You may need to ignite a controlled burn at this point to get real alignment. Orchestrated conflict plays an important role in many decision processes.

The idea that we can get a room full of smart, dedicated people who do totally different things to agree on everything is a bit silly – and, honestly, not desirable. If our ideas and direction go untested and everyone seems to agree, this is a bad sign. It means we're missing something, we lack diversity or people are having 'half conversations' and not contributing openly.

This needs to be safe, so make it fun. When I'm working with groups that have deeply entrenched positions, I'll often run a mock 'debate' filled with laughter and frivolity to safely poke them into experimenting with different perspectives.

Alignment is not about agreement – it's about productive disagreement that enables a consensus. With productive disagreement, we expose all the different perspectives we're grappling with and put them on the table. We don't need to resolve all our differences, but we do need to take a peek from every angle, find the grey areas and agree on how to manage them.

Find a safe way to argue. Build humour and absurdity into your conversation. Spark a ludicrous moot and stage a formal debate, ask people for their worst or most offensive idea and encourage lateral thinking. Start with something external or non-work-related if you have to, but get that muscle moving!

STAY SCEPTICAL

Early in my business, I specialised in developing business cases for big spends like new facilities or digital transformation. When we ran the numbers we would always apply an optimism bias, building additional time or cost into our projections to counter the tendency to undercook estimates.

Even experts are overly optimistic when they plan. We underestimate costs, underestimate risk and overestimate how much we can deliver, even in the face of information to the contrary. It's why nine out of 10 people think they're an above-average driver, and why the average house build goes over budget by 10 to 30 per cent. For standard building projects, the optimism bias is anywhere from 5 to 50 per cent for how long it will take, and 25 to 200 per cent for how much it will cost. For technology and transformation projects, it's even more.

Good business case development doesn't stop at a self-imposed optimism bias, though. We need to get out of our own heads, and have our budgets and schedule reviewed by an external third party – what Daniel Kahneman calls 'The Outside View'. Testing for holes with an independent eye is a powerful way to get a reality check and spot gaps. It's why books have a proofreader and boards include independent experts – when we're too close for something, we often miss essential bits.

This is about accepting dependence on other things, too – external factors, other projects, other people – and recognising that points of potential failure are likely outside of our control. With this perspective, preparing to be wrong isn't a personal indictment; it's just an acceptance of how the world is.

Evaluation should consider more than our criteria – which are usually best-case oriented – and include a range of potential impacts and scenarios, including what might go wrong.

Take the time to ask:

- What might go wrong?
- Is this realistic?
- Have we tested this with the right people?

GIVE IT A CRACK

At a recent conference, I interviewed a prominent Australian mayor to profile his council's pioneering work in digitally driven cities. When I asked him which conditions most enabled his success, he confidently answered, 'We have a culture that makes it OK to fail'. So far, so good. The wheels came off a bit when I asked him a follow-up question: 'Can you tell us about a time that you've failed?'

Silence.

Making it OK to fail is one of the war cries of the new leadership movement, but it seems very focused on other people. Our senior leaders' willingness to experiment is still woeful.

With the pace of change, disciplined experimentation must take the place of carefully planned execution. When we're in unchartered territory, we generally need to have a go before we understand enough to decide on a suitable response.

When I work with leadership teams, I often ask them to commit to the practice of 90-day trials, where they launch a new idea or pilot every quarter. Building the expectation of iteration and change into our work programme takes the pressure off and creates a culture of experimentation. Never make a big commitment when you can make a small one. In all decision processes, we need to find the safest, minimum viable way to test our ideas.

Incorporate pilots, experiments and testing into your decision journey before asking for a final commitment. Stay curious about all the ways you're wrong that you haven't realised yet, and embrace those lessons with gratitude and triumph as you track towards your final choice.

What we've learned so far

- Thinking should happen in groups whenever possible.
- Our initial frame sets the scene for how we think about our problems.
- Creating a safe space means asking who, when, how and what.
- Making a decision asks us to ideate, evaluate and stay sceptical.
- Never make a big decision when you can make a small one.

Your next step

Consider the most important decision you have coming up. How can you involve others to improve your outcomes?

LESSON 8

Decisions are like babies

My eldest daughter turns 16 this year. Looking back on her childhood, it's interesting to think about how my perspective has changed over time. As a new mother, I assumed that by age 18 my children would be somewhat… 'done'. Once they'd learned all the skills they needed at home, I'd have ready-to-go adults who'd venture out into the world prepared. I also assumed that as they got older, they'd need less input from me.

Naïve, eh? As a former foster kid with no parental input in my adult life, I didn't realise how valuable that connection is. As my children grow, it's becoming clear that they will likely never stop needing their parents.

Like real babies, decision babies are rarely ever 'done'.

When it comes to big decisions, the lifespan can be long. As things change, our environment shifts and we try new things; we're never really done. Remember: decisions are rarely a linear process. They're iterative, so every decision is informed by previous ones.

Just like babies, decisions grow up and usually have babies of their own – informed by the past and guided by the future.

Committing to your decision baby means they're alive, but not finished. Very few decisions meet all their objectives and avoid all unintended consequences – especially on the first go. We're not aiming for perfect – if we've found it, the odds are that we're missing something. What we *are* aiming to do is keep tweaking, shifting and changing as new information comes to light, and we understand all the unexpected ways we were wrong.

Being a decisive leader isn't about digging in your heels no matter what - that's a character-driven story. It's about having the right skills to pick a path no matter what happens in the arena.

In *Essentialism*, Greg McKeown talks about reaching the highest point of contribution. He defines this as doing the right thing, at the right time, for the right reason. Good decision-making meets all of those criteria, but it needs a couple of other things too: the right people, with the right attitude.

Miss just one or two of these ingredients and the quality of our decisions suffers. Strategic leaders test their thinking relentlessly, asking tricky questions about whether their choices make sense.

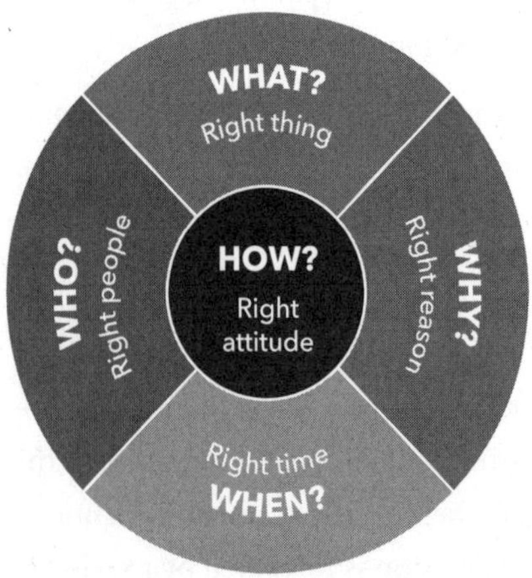

THE RIGHT THING

Doing the right thing is all about context and how we frame our choices – the 'where'. Action and detail-oriented leaders have a strong temptation to jump into options before taking the time to understand what's going on. But without a clear understanding of our context, we can't be sure we're solving the right problem – or that a problem even exists.

Here are some questions we might ask to determine whether we're doing the right thing:

- Does the problem exist?
- Could we think about this differently?
- Do we need to solve this?
- How important is this, in light of our broader context?

THE RIGHT REASON

Doing things for the right reason is about outcomes and the value we're trying to add. It's the 'why'. If we aren't motivated by the right outcomes, it's hard to make the right choices. Making a good decision means we need to be clear about the change we're trying to make in the world, and make sure our choices align to that motivation.

Here are some questions we might ask to examine the motivations behind our decisions:

- Who benefits from this decision – and who suffers?
- What outcomes are we trying to achieve?
- What flow-on effects haven't we considered?
- What are the costs and risks if we don't act?

THE RIGHT PEOPLE

Involving the right people is all about the human element of decision-making – the 'who'. Nothing is more frustrating than failing to get the right people on your side. Worse still is when you embark on a course of action without the skills, capability or mandate to act – this sets you up for failure from the beginning.

Here are some questions we might ask to test whether we have the right people on board:

- What capability is needed?
- Do we have the right skills?
- Who should be involved?
- Do we have a mandate?

THE RIGHT TIME

Timing is all about feasibility – the 'when'. Without a sense of urgency, it's difficult to mobilise people to action – and rightly so! There are more than enough problems waiting to be solved, and if things aren't done in the right order, we pay an opportunity cost for diluting our attention in other areas.

For those with a bias towards action, it can be hard to wait, but not everything needs doing right now. Plenty of failed inventions were ahead of their time. Microsoft invented a doomed tablet a decade before Apple released the iPad. AT&T developed a 'Picturephone' in 1964, decades before FaceTime and Skype became popular – but the public, infrastructure and supporting systems weren't ready for it. Get your timing wrong, and it doesn't matter how good your idea is.

Here are some questions we might ask about dependencies and sequencing:

- Why now?
- What else is going on?
- Are we ready?
- Are they ready?

THE RIGHT ATTITUDE

Having the right attitude is all about commitment to outcomes, not solutions. Commitment to solutions sees us become narrow-minded and stubborn. Commitment to outcomes fosters openness and innovation. We need to understand and challenge our internal biases and come in with an open and curious mindset. Unless you're aware of what you're thinking in the first place, it's pretty tough to think differently.

Staying open to experimentation is critical here. We need the opportunity to make minimum viable decisions before committing to the long haul. Often this is about identifying the smallest possible step we can take, to discover all the ways we're wrong.

Here are some questions we might ask to assess whether we have the right attitude:

- Do we care?
- Are we open to exploring?
- Are our options realistic or just superficial?
- Are we motivated by outcomes, or simply committed to a solution?

What we've learned so far

- Decisions are like babies – never finished and likely to spawn new ones.
- We need to check we're doing the right thing, for the right reason, with the right people, at the right time, with the right attitude.

Your next step

Evaluate a decision you've made recently against the five criteria. How does it stack up? How could you tweak it to keep it relevant?

CHEAT SHEET

DECISIONS

What we've learned

We need to bring thinking back in-house. Making good decisions is about how we think, not what we think. No high-priced consultant can give you the perfect answer, because really, there isn't one. Instead, we need to focus on the process of our decision-making. Like babies, decisions are never really done, and if we can't build our own strategic capability we open ourselves up to risk and close off new possibilities.

While doubtful leaders opt out of the thinking process, decisive leaders lean into it. Instead of trying to be right all the time, land on the answer quickly and point fingers at people when things go wrong, the decisive leader is more open. While they're careful to set the right frame, they put their attention into the process – engaging with people, challenging assumptions safely and experimenting with options and ideas by making the minimum viable decision.

Here are a few attributes of doubtful versus decisive leaders:

Doubtful leaders	Decisive leaders
Set the tone	Set the frame
Look for certainty	Look for clarity
Challenge people	Challenge assumptions
Drive decision-making	Create a safe space
Limit discussion	Generate ideas
Rush to an answer	Experiment with options
Hedge and relitigate	Commit to action

What you can do

To make better decisions, you don't need a strategy MBA or to be super-intelligent. Intelligence, like promotion, can hold us back, because we develop a disproportionate perspective on the quality of our thinking. And even if you *are* right, it doesn't necessarily matter. Change is a team sport, so decision-making needs to be, too. Without access to collective intelligence, even the best decisions won't have any impact.

Practise your thinking skills. Create deliberate space away from the busywork. Clear time in your calendar, schedule big-picture conversations and start to nudge the culture of your team or organisation away from what's directly in front of them.

For your next big decision, think carefully about the process you'd like to use to make it – who do you need involved? What criteria will you use to decide the right path? How will you test your ideas? You don't need to be the decision-maker to have a positive impact on the process. Sometimes asking a few more tricky questions is all that's needed.

Reflect on some of the decisions you've made that haven't gone well, using the five criteria in lesson 8 to see how they stack up. Was the timing wrong? Did you fail to get the right people on board? Were your motivations off?

Most importantly, keep asking tricky questions. Every time something makes sense, poke it with a stick – are you sure about that? How do you know? Could something else be true?

Three key questions

1. Why does this matter?
2. How do we choose?
3. What's the smallest experiment we can try?

MODULE 3

SYSTEMS

For when you need to make things work

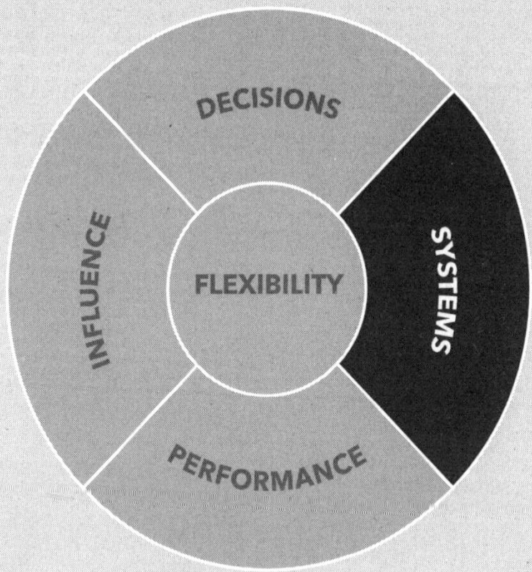

LESSONS IN THIS MODULE

9. Heroes beat the odds, but systems change them
10. Don't solve problems, dissolve them
11. Put your money where your mouth is

LESSON 9

Heroes beats the odds, but systems change them

I used to think I was such a hero. (Truthfully, I often still do.) In my childhood, I learned that the only person I could ever truly depend on was me. My mother was unpredictable, my family was fractured and anyone I ever came to depend on in the years that followed – government agencies, foster families, relationships and friends – inevitably let me down. Those deeply embedded patterns have followed me through my life and career in unhelpful ways, becoming a reinforcing story that I perpetuate without realising it.

Every time someone else dropped the ball, I'd swoop in and save the day. I worked more hours, did more stuff and ticked more boxes than anyone else. If you want something done right, you do it yourself… right?

Wrong. You can't be trusted alone. The hero model always starts off great – for bootstrappers, self-made people and start-ups especially – but once you get through the initial madness, it becomes a risky strategy. Heroes get hooked on the buzz and start to experience cognitive dissonance. We don't see the balls we're dropping, the risks we're taking or the limitations of our efforts. When you're the white knight that saves the day, always pulling off the impossible, you start to believe in and rely on the fairytale. Over time, like my fear of trusting others, it becomes a story that's hard to shift – and it holds us back.

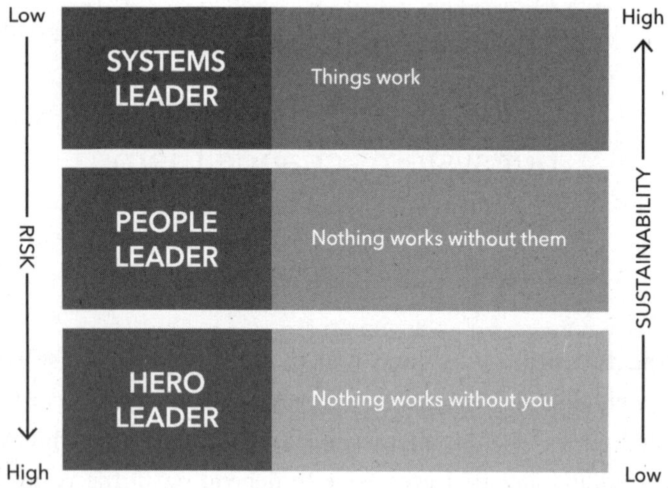

If we can't stop thinking of ourselves as irreplaceable, we get stuck. Most leaders, by virtue of promotion or realisation, start to figure that out eventually, so they learn to delegate, becoming people leaders. This is a great start – when heroes redirect their energy into leading people, they reduce the single point of risk and spread it more thinly across a team. More points of failure, sure, but more diversification.

While heroes beat the odds, *systems change them*. Here's a test: how much do you know about Reed Hastings? Anything?

…What about Netflix?

Reed Hastings, the founding CEO of Netflix, isn't an amazing leader because he's a hero, but because he built an powerful and unique system for content and video streaming. Netflix changed the way people experience entertainment, the way content is created and, you could argue, the way people live.

Examples of systems leaders are rife throughout history, but sometimes we confuse them with heroes. Nelson Mandela isn't a hero because he worked so hard, but because he instigated the systems change that overturned apartheid. Richard Branson isn't a hero because he's at work longer than anyone else or hires the best people, but because he developed systems that changed the way industries work – from music production to air travel.

Systems leadership is the undiscovered frontier in leadership that counts, and it's a completely different kettle of fish from what we're taught in an MBA. Systems leaders see differently. They focus on how all the puzzle pieces fit together and join them up in a unique way.

When we think in systems, how much we know, how hard we work and how good our people are become less important. Systems help us create new ways of thinking and working the default. Systems leaders set up their environment to maximise success, *even when people are fallible.*

Systems make our success sustainable. When we understand the way our business runs and we build robust systems, things change. We reduce dependence on key people, decrease risk and save time and money. And thanks to that, we boost productivity and performance.

MAKE WORK WORK

A system is a combination of different parts that work together to make things happen. It's both very simple and totally confusing. Most people and organisations use the singular and plural of the word for different contexts – that is: 'the System' and 'systems'. Let's take a look at the differences between the two:

The System	Systems
How everything fits together	Processes, tools and workflows
Zoomed out	Zoomed in

'The System', singular, describes how everything fits together. We talk about 'the System' when we're zooming out to talk about the way a whole sector, organisation or team functions. That is how I will use it here, too. For clarity, when I'm talking about the System, I'll capitalise it.

When we talk about 'systems', plural, we're talking about the processes and tools used to get things done – like workflows and software infrastructure.

The System is the way everything fits together. Your systems are the building blocks of your organisation or team, enabling you to achieve a goal or solve a problem. Done well, systems do the heavy lifting for us, by creating an environment that makes it easier to do the right thing than the wrong thing.

Systems are ways of working that make it easier for the System to achieve its goals.

BUILD A BETTER HOUSE

Imagine trying to train a horse to run faster by teaching each of its legs to perform more efficiently. Dumb, right? Yet, decades after Michael Ballé first used this analogy in his book *Managing with Systems Thinking*, we continue to design organisations that do exactly that. The result is an environment that produces *less than* the sum of its five best-practice parts.

The core parts of the System differ depending on the type and size of your organisation, but usually include functions such as communication, finance, customer service, people and culture, delivery and operations. All of these parts have their own 'work' – the inputs they need to do a good job and the outputs they deliver. These are essential components for the system to function, but on their own they are insufficient, or even irrelevant.

Your organisation is not the sum of its interconnected parts. It is the product of the *relationships* between those parts. Improving each part separately does not guarantee the improvement of the performance of the whole – in fact, it can do the opposite. As Draper L Kauffman says, dividing a cow in half does not give us two smaller cows:

> *You may end up with a lot of hamburger, but the essential nature of 'cow' – a living system capable, among other things, of turning grass into milk – then would be lost. A system functions as a 'whole'. Its behavior depends on its entire structure and not just on adding up the behavior of its different pieces.*

Most organisational problems are better solved somewhere other than where they appear. A systems view focuses on relationships. The architect knows this clearly, drawing the house first, then the rooms. Rooms are only improved in ways that enhance the house. If the room can be made worse to make the whole house better, it will be.

Signs you need to tackle your systems

- You keep finding the same problems in different places.
- Performance depends on the efforts of individuals.
- Things take longer or feel harder than they should.

Is your team or organisation too focused on the individual parts, rather than relationships between them?

MAKE THE RIGHT THING THE EASY THING

In *Factfulness*, Hans Rosling talks about the difference between the EU's commitment to the Geneva Convention and EU policy as it applies to refugees. In 2015, 4000 refugees, many of whom were escaping deadly conflict in Syria, drowned in the Mediterranean Sea as they tried to reach Europe in inflatable boats. The world watched in horror at images of bodies, including many children, washing up on European holiday beaches.

How did this happen? All the countries they were heading to were signatories to the Geneva Convention, where refugees are entitled to seek asylum. It wasn't a matter of resources: passage on a dodgy boat costs up to 20 times as much as a plane fare from Turkey or Libya, where most of the boats left from. It wasn't a capacity issue, either: there were plenty of seats available on the appropriate flights.

The problem was at the check-in counter, where airline staff stopped refugees from boarding planes without appropriate documentation. This isn't because airlines are bad, or the staff were evil – it was a system requirement. A European Council Directive from 2001, aimed at combating immigration, requires that any airline or ferry company that allows an undocumented person into Europe is liable for the costs of returning that person to their country of origin.

While that directive is explicit about excluding refugees, as defined by the Geneva Convention, that meant little to airline check-in staff who are not trained to assess whether someone qualifies for asylum-seeker status. The safest option for the airlines, and their staff, was to ensure that nobody boarded a plane without a visa.

So, with air travel unavailable, refugees must travel by sea. But why in such dodgy vessels? More regulatory madness. All boats are confiscated on arrival, so they can only be used for one trip. That means that smugglers can't afford to use safe or quality vessels.

On the face of it, European governments are committed to supporting asylum seekers. But in practice, the misaligned policies, practices and systems that could enable that commitment are supporting a market of smugglers and directly contributing to thousands of avoidable deaths.

This high-stakes example of systems failure demonstrates that when we don't design our systems correctly, we can't achieve our goals, no matter how committed to them we might be. In fact, when we don't design our systems well, we make it *harder* for good stuff to happen.

Do you have policies, processes or procedures that make it harder to achieve your goals? How could you change that?

DEFAULTS ARE DANGEROUS

When you start a new job, you have fresh eyes. Have you ever entered a new environment and felt baffled by the way some things are done? As a newbie, you see things that many long-serving staff no longer notice or think about. You turn over rocks that have sat still for years, questioning things that don't make sense.

That stage doesn't last. The longer we do something, the more normal it seems. Even though things keep changing in our teams and our environment, we develop blind spots. Within six months, you're another cog in the wheel, perpetrating the default along with everyone else.

Whether by accident or by design, every team and organisation settles into a default way of doing things.

Yesterday's adaptations are today's routines.

Heifetz, Linsky and Grashow

Defaults aren't inherently negative – they serve the job we once needed them to. But if we don't question them regularly, the consequences can be devastating. Systems underpin more than just the way we work. After a while, they drive the way we think. Left unchecked, defaults can create an organisational culture we didn't intend.

In 2019, the New Zealand Labour government's much-awaited Wellbeing Budget sparked a furore – but not for the reasons the government had hoped. On Tuesday 28 May, two days before the official launch, the Opposition released sensitive details about what would be included in the Budget – and the government went into a tailspin.

Then Secretary to the Treasury Gabriel Makhlouf was quick to comment, striking fear into the hearts of CIOs and conspiracists across New Zealand. Treasury's systems, he told the media gravely, had been 'deliberately and systematically hacked' and the police had been notified.

Finance Minister Grant Robertson went one step further that afternoon, letting the media know the government had contacted the National Party about the police investigation – subtly implying the Opposition was responsible for the hack. The Opposition kicked back, accusing the government of a smear campaign and calling for heads to roll.

Just a day and a half later, on Budget morning, Gabriel Makhlouf was subdued as he explained to the media that they hadn't been hacked after all. The sensitive material, it turned out, was readily available on Treasury's website. The Opposition 'hackers' weren't cyber geniuses – they'd just used the search engine for its intended function. The Budget was available, lawfully, to anyone who searched for it, and it had been like this, unchecked, for years.

On Friday of that week, I headed into Treasury to speak to a group of government change managers on engagement and influence. Travelling with my Australian videographer, who was pulling a large suitcase full of camera gear behind him, I wondered aloud what kind of security we'd encounter at the door.

At reception, I was greeted by a friendly face. After explaining who I was, the receptionist exclaimed 'Oh! Great! Right down here'. To our surprise and amusement, she proceeded to scan her ID card, open the office door and wave her hand vaguely towards the corridor. 'You'll need to go down there and find the meeting room.' No sign-in, no identity check. Very well, maybe we'd been pre-authorised somehow.

After wrapping up my presentation, I lingered to mingle with some of the audience members. At the third person, I did a double take when I saw her name tag. Quickly glancing behind to check I hadn't been mistaken, I confirmed: this was the third Christine I'd spoken to in five minutes.

Interrupting the woman in front of me, I queried, 'Sorry, I can't help but notice – you're the third Christine I've spoken to here – is something going on? Either all change managers are called Christine, or…' The woman broke into laughter. 'I know it's funny, isn't it? We all turned up in a big group, so the receptionist just swiped her ID card and hit 'print' a bunch of times!'

Between me, my videographer and the change managers in attendance, more than 50 unidentified people were milling around inside Treasury. Budget leak notwithstanding, the implications for health, safety and security in New Zealand's earthquake capital were no joke.

The results of a public inquiry into the Budget leak were made available early in 2020, and the report was clear in its findings. Shortfalls in assurance processes had contributed to technical decisions that led to the website design fault, and a lack of action in response to security concerns. More generally, the risk management system inside Treasury was inadequate, and governance and oversight at all levels throughout the agency fell short of expected standards.

Colour me surprised. The Budget 'leak' and my reception experience were not unrelated incidents, nor were they the result of individual failure – they're how systems function. In Treasury, the same sorts of problems could be found everywhere, and performance relied on the competence of individuals. Those weaknesses eventually led to an attention-grabbing breakdown – but the Budget leak wasn't the first or only example of assurance failure, as the inquiry revealed.

Deeply entrenched systems are invisible, tenacious, and embedded – they become 'the way we do things around here', and can be difficult to notice. Systems become enmeshed with structures, norms and culture, and it can be hard to see room for change or improvement.

What are you not seeing anymore? Do the same crimes appear everywhere?

Each piece of the puzzle is connected to everything else, and part of a larger, stronger force that isn't always comfortable or safe to talk about. Multiply those conflicts and tensions across dozens, hundreds or thousands of people and the potential for resistance becomes exponential. So, where do you start? How do you begin to untangle the web, find the friction points and open people to a better future?

You ask them how.

ASK BETTER QUESTIONS

Organisational drag is a chronic source of friction, making things harder and more time-consuming than they should be – and it's mostly invisible. Today's knowledge workers spend 80 to 85 per cent of their time in meetings, yet leaders consistently get their estimates of meeting time wrong by at least 50 per cent. We're all so busy pushing barrows and pointing fingers at each other for going too slow that we can't appreciate the weight of the load.

You don't need complicated software or an expensive consultant to diagnose systems issues; you just need to listen to the people who are held back by them. Most workplaces make a token effort to do so via their annual engagement survey, but unless the results come out positive the feedback gets minimised or disregarded. Even when people accurately and consistently pinpoint the things that make their jobs hard, they get ignored – or, worse, accused of whinging or failing to perform. This is a mistake.

Study after study shows that while employees desperately want to be productive, their workplace is getting in the way. The average organisation loses more than a day a week to undetected organisational drag. Systems leaders are attuned to this and rather than blaming others, they listen, spot the themes and join the dots.

We need to ask three critical questions to diagnose systems:

1. Why?
2. So what?
3. Is it, though?

And we need to keep asking them, until we find the real crime.

Systems: a case study

Consider this large government agency frustrated by technology procurement. The chief technology officer was beside himself. The policy was clear: the tablet of choice in this organisation was a Microsoft Surface Pro. The Surface Pro fit neatly into the organisation's wider software and hardware ecosystem, had the specifications engineers and other workers needed to do their work, and the software was well-supported. But despite a clear organisational directive on technology purchasing, staff kept buying unauthorised iPads.

They'd done everything they could think of to make Surface Pros the easy choice: negotiating a bulk purchase deal, creating training and support videos and manuals that were easily accessible, and making the ordering process as speedy and straightforward as possible.

The unauthorised iPads were causing the IT team serious grief, with complicated technical support, security risks and expensive maintenance and repairs. What could they do?

Start with why

Our first step in getting to the bottom of this issue was diagnosis. We had to get out in the field and dig a little deeper. We started with one of the engineering team leaders. Here's how the conversation went:

> ***Us: Why do people keep buying iPads?***
>
> *Engineering team leader: Microsoft Surface Pro doesn't support our field assessment software.*

Oh. Oops. That was a reasonably easy answer – and we could have stopped there. But we didn't.

> ***Us: Why did we choose a tablet that wouldn't support field assessment?***
>
> *Information systems manager: When we first bought the Surface Pros and adopted the technology policy, we didn't know they would need to be used to perform field assessments. We can't do anything about it now, either. We're locked into using Surface Pros for the next three years.*

Uh oh. Well, that's the end of that, right? Wrong.

> ***Us: Why did we buy a solution that wasn't fit for our future needs, and why did we lock ourselves in?***
>
> *Digital procurement manager: We didn't talk to the engineering team when we developed our digital strategy, and we didn't know health and safety legislation was about*

to change. We locked in for three years because that was the cheapest whole-of-life solution, which our business unit KPIs require.

That's three 'whys', and we've got some good systems-focused answers here. If we chose to, we could head off and look at options for changing our structure and making procurement more flexible. That would be an excellent move and deliver significantly more value than if we'd stopped at the first why. For fun, though, we kept going.

Us: Why is our digital strategy and incentive structure so out of sync with our organisational needs?

Chief technology officer: We don't engage with the wider organisation when we prepare and test our strategy. In this situation we were under huge time pressure, and there are some big silos here that make it hard to get other people involved. Even when we invite people from other business units to meetings, they don't come, or they don't contribute.

OK, now we're really getting somewhere. Let's poke some more.

Us: Why don't your people want to engage across different business units?

Group of middle managers: They're all overwhelmed just doing their day jobs – and there's no real incentive to. We assess our performance at a business unit level on financial results and technical performance. Those indicators go down to the individual performance assessments, too, and with the last two restructures, people are terrified to do anything that would compromise those results.

Five 'whys' deep, and suddenly we have some rich, systemic answers to our iPad problem. We knew we'd struck gold when we hit on an issue that didn't just have one flow-on effect – in this case, technology purchasing – but was popping up all over the place. Then, in a one-hour session with middle managers, we found out that silos weren't just a problem for the technology team – they were creating issues across the entire organisation.

In this siloed agency, we'd encountered a common problem: an organisation that was trying to make the racehorse run faster by working on each leg individually.

We couldn't fix the whole world after our investigation. Changing deeper systemic issues was scheduled for discussion at the next executive team meeting, where the chief technology officer would table a report on performance management, prepared in collaboration with the people and capability general manager.

In the meantime, we had an excellent diagnosis of the targeted problems at each of our 'why' levels, and the things we could shift to improve them. Potential systems changes included:

- A new plan for the technology team to engage with the wider business
- Guidance for teams on how to develop and test digital strategy
- A review of vendor contract formats and rules, in collaboration with procurement
- A capability review for the technology team, assessing liaison and strategic capacity
- A shift in performance measurement at the business unit and individual level.

Taking a systems lens and continuing to ask 'why' had shifted our understanding of the problem from people to systems.

Systems diagnosis is about more than problem-solving, though, and requires us to consider the *impact* of our choices. For this, we went to the technology team and asked: 'So what?'

Question the impact

Remember – the original problem was that people kept buying iPads when there was a clear policy against it. The organisation mandated Microsoft Surface Pros because they linked to the overarching software ecosystem, and they had the technical support available easily and cheaply. But people kept buying iPads. Let's do the 'So what?' test.

> ***Us: So what if people keep buying iPads?***
>
> *Technology team: It's not consistent across the organisation.*
>
> ***Us: So what if we're not consistent?***
>
> *Technology team: When we're not consistent, it makes technical support more expensive and complicated, and it opens a security risk.*
>
> ***Us: So what if it's expensive and risky?***
>
> *Technology team: It's irresponsible public management! We run up big costs, and when we have security risks it puts people's privacy at stake. When we take risks with performance, it damages our reputation.*
>
> ***Us: Ah. So what are we really trying to protect, then?***
>
> *Technology team: Value, security, privacy, performance and reputation.*
>
> ***Us: So... what could we change?***
>
> *Technology team: The way we do tech support, to make it less expensive to troubleshoot multiple platforms.*
>
> *Our security environment, to make it easier to protect data and privacy with non-regulation applications and software.*
>
> *Our programme planning, to integrate with project teams at the beginning of a project to identify the best technology solutions to avoid problems down the line.*

In this example, we encouraged the technology team to use their agency to think about what *they* could do, even if they couldn't change others' behaviours. By understanding what was driving the key risks and consequences, the team could take action.

Both lines of questioning had yielded rich, useful data and tips about how the organisation could redesign its systems to kill its problems in the egg and manage impact more effectively. We weren't done there, though. Advanced systems leaders dig through another layer, examining the assumptions that sit underneath the answers to all of our 'whys' and 'so whats'.

Challenge assumptions

For the final step in our diagnosis of the Great iPad Problem, we got the technology team, engineering supervisors and middle managers together and spent an hour unpicking some of the underlying assumptions we might have made. We pulled out our third question: 'is it, though?'

Teams were permitted to ask each other curly questions and look for the holes in each other's thinking. Together, we challenged each other and filled a whiteboard, asking questions like:

- Is it really such a security risk?
- Would using a different software really affect performance?
- Do people really need to do field assessments?
- Is it really IT's job to be doing all the tech support? Should it be?

By the end, we had new ideas for how each of our stakeholders could do their work to make the whole process easier, simpler and safer. We also had new options to consider around the technology team's operating model, contracts, and procurement and competency frameworks. More importantly, we'd developed a deeper understanding of how the System worked together and how the organisation's most important relationships functioned. We'd built trust and created a connection that everyone in the room could draw on in the future.

If we'd left the problem statement unexamined, we would have just tightened the controls or consequences for buying iPads. Trust and engagement across the business would have worsened, and people still would have found a way to buy iPads. The problem would have become less visible, as people quietly went around the rules, making it more likely that security and performance issues would go unchecked until they created a bigger problem.

The lesson here is this: when you've made it as easy as possible to do the right thing and people still aren't doing it, it probably *isn't* the right thing. People take the easiest path available to them to meet their objectives. If they're taking a different path to the one you want, then yours is not the easiest way.

What problems are you trying to solve that need you to ask better questions about?

What we've learned so far

- Heroes are a risk.
- There's no such thing as a single crime.
- Defaults are dangerous.
- We need to ask better questions.
- The right thing should be the easy thing.

Your next step

Consider some of the biggest challenges in your team and ask three critical questions:

1. Why?
2. So what?
3. Is it though?

Keep asking them until you hit the root cause.

LESSON 10

Don't solve problems, dissolve them

The real goal of problem-solving shouldn't be to solve a problem. It should be to *dissolve* it by changing our environment so that the problem can no longer exist.

When we've done a good job of diagnosing our problems, our instinct is to jump straight to a solution: the tools we can buy and processes we can change. But systems aren't what you *buy*, or what you *do* – they're how things *work*. To get that right, we need to park our desire to buy a system and design one instead.

FIND THE WEAKEST LINK

In vintage management opus *The Goal* we meet Jonah – a factory manager who struggles to understand why his factories aren't making money. He quickly realises that the easiest way to improve productivity isn't to expand capacity, as first suspected, but to work out what is really blocking his manufacturing chain. By zooming out, he was able to zoom all the way in. This is the essence of strategic systems design. We *zoom out* to see how the System works – our team, organisation, factory, sector or community – and then *zoom in* on the elements of the process that are causing the biggest issues.

Netflix zoomed out to look at how people lived, interacted and consumed entertainment content, and then zoomed in on the bottleneck that made things the hardest – inconsistent and expensive access to programming that didn't fit people's personal schedules. Netflix didn't start life as a content-creating, video streaming monolith. Instead, it recognised the most significant point of failure – late fees for videos and DVDs – and addressed that first. Between 2000 and 2007, Netflix was primarily a mail-out DVD service that gave people agency over when they watched what they paid for. Over a number of years, as their market and the overall technology landscape evolved, they expanded that principle into today's empire, offering on-demand access to a full range of quality content.

Like Netflix, we don't want to fix everything at once. We want to identify the most significant point of failure and focus on eliminating that first. Often, when the big rocks move, the little ones begin to take care of themselves. That means we don't necessarily need to fix the most complicated problems, but focus our attention on the link in the chain that's causing the most grief.

It's easy to get distracted in the process of problem-finding – there always seems to be so many. Luckily, most of them don't matter. The key is to focus on the *purpose* of our system, because not all things need improving for the sake of it. As Jonah wryly points out in the movie version of *The Goal*, companies aren't built to show off their efficiencies.

The capacity of the plant is equal to the
capacity of its bottlenecks.

Eliyahu M Goldratt, *The Goal*

To find the weakest link, we need to zoom out by having the right conversations with the right people. Then we need to zoom in, optimising our attention and aiming for small, significant change.

SEE THE BIG PICTURE

When you start trying to design a new system or process, the easiest way to see all your different relationships and dependencies is usually in picture form – like those below.

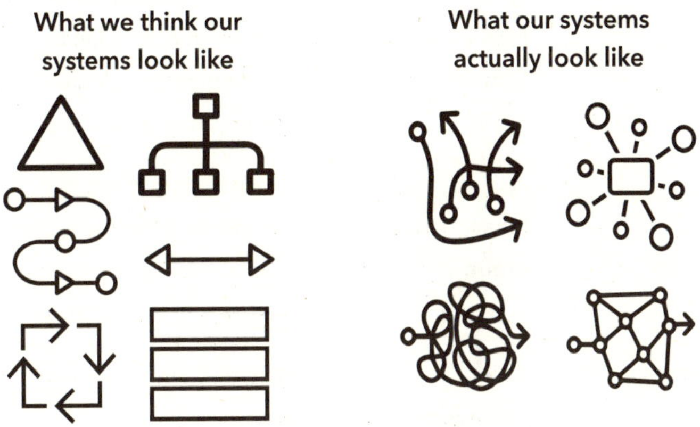

While there is an incredible array of digital mapping tools available, every systems leader should be comfortable drawing up their systems manually.

The bigger the paper or whiteboard, the better. Start rough and expect to make a mess by kicking off a hands-on brain dump. Here's how I suggest tackling it.

Purpose

Start by identifying the purpose of the System. Write the goal at the top or in the middle and make sure it's prominent throughout the entire process. Remember: we don't build organisations to create efficiencies, we build organisations to achieve a goal.

Every system (whether it's a capital or lower-case 's') needs to have a clear purpose, but what that looks like will depend on whether we're considering the System, a system, a part, a process or a relationship.

Take a local government asset management process, for example. Here's how the purpose might vary along the chain:

		System purpose
The System	Nice Place City Council	To improve quality of life for people who live in our local community, now and in the future.
Part	Infrastructure group	To provide the infrastructure that enables our community's quality of life, now and in the future.
Process	Asset management	To make good infrastructure decisions.
Relationship 1	Finance department	To ensure our infrastructure decisions offer value for money.
Relationship 2	Strategy department	To ensure our infrastructure decisions align with strategic priorities and community needs.

Consider how many nested purposes might sit underneath our process (the gathering, processing or reporting of information, capital works planning or quality control), and how many different relationships might be involved. Consider, too, what might happen when we start looking at the purpose of various tools, capabilities and people involved in our system.

Each nested purpose statement should be linked by a common thread – alignment to the purpose of the big picture, or the System. If we can't see the link all the way up, we're in trouble – and that's when we start focusing on the wrong things.

Place

Around the edges of your paper, identify all the different environmental factors that affect the System. These might be regulatory change, market shifts, customer demand or technology changes. Or, perhaps, upcoming elections, a scandal faced by a recent competitor or an emerging lifestyle trend.

Parts

Next, identify all the different parts of the System. Draw or scribble every contributing aspect you can think of, and tag them using words, pictures, symbols and colours. Draw the key people who work in each part as stick figures, giving them names and titles as you go.

Processes

Continue to resist the temptation for order, and start drawing arrows, loops and lines between all of your different parts, to show the relationships and processes between each. Remember: relationships are messy, so your map probably will be, too.

Prioritise

Now that you've zoomed out, you can look at each of your system's parts and processes in detail, with the goal of stripping out or simplifying as many steps as possible. Work through your messy map, highlight or circle the steps that make up the critical path, and signal which parts look like they might be optional.

Now, start again

Now you can start with a fresh piece of paper and begin to build a new version of your overall system. Identify opportunities to optimise, delete, change and invest, and test your thinking with others. Sometimes things don't need to go – they just need to change order, or reduce in size.

Generally, we end up with a combination of approaches – some things move, some are optimised, some are deleted and some are added. For Nice Place City Council, for example, a systems audit might see:

- The strategy department *change the timing* of the annual strategic planning process to reduce rework for finance and infrastructure
- The finance department *streamline and optimise* their annual budgeting by working in more effectively with the strategic planning process, and aligning their delegations and approvals policy to match
- The infrastructure department *invest in* asset management software and data analytics to feed more accurate information into both processes each year and reduce manual calculations.

Each of these system changes focuses on the relationships between parts and processes, rather than the benefit to the individual business group. In a siloed workplace, they're difficult to identify, but when the system is seen in its entirety, these changes have the potential to transform the effectiveness of the entire organisation.

ASK THE RIGHT PEOPLE

Every step in this process needs the involvement or input of the people who are involved in, use or are affected by your system, to make sure you're not missing important information. When we don't take account of the relationships between parts, and the reality of the frontline, we risk hamstringing the results of entire teams, programmes or organisations.

I watched this happen in a government agency once. It was notorious for working in siloes, despite preaching community collaboration and partnership. One of its key teams was dedicated to supporting communities to shape their own futures – putting together projects, running initiatives and getting their neighbours together. This is great stuff – until you're one of the community groups that wants to be involved, and you find out that the red tape requires a formal constitution, charitable status and $2 million in public liability insurance.

Oops.

In this situation the finance, risk and procurement teams hadn't done anything wrong – they were doing all the right, best-practice things. But when it came to actually supporting communities to shape their own futures, their decisions were way out of step.

Making good stuff happen is hard enough at the best of times, but it's close to impossible when the way we do business directly undermines our goals and intentions. Eliminating real friction means aligning every aspect of our operations to the goal we're trying to achieve.

The policy wonks among you will be familiar with the concept of a 'nudge'. The rest of you might enjoy the appropriately titled book by Thaler and Sunstein. The idea is this: it's much easier to influence people's behaviour by providing an environment that supports good choices than to rely on agency, willpower or sheer determination. In large organisations, this environment depends largely on the work of our back office or 'internal teams'.

Internal teams – like HR, legal, finance, customer service, ICT, research, policy and other support functions – are the most underutilised system design tool in any organisation. They are the engine room of sustainable change – yet, because they aren't doing the fancy public-facing work or the strategic stuff, they often don't see themselves reflected in goals and strategies. Instead, they content themselves with getting on with 'doing the work'. This is a mistake.

We can't stop with our internal teams, though – they don't know what it's like on the ground. Good systems design brings in the designers, and the doers.

In a former life, I used to help put together tender responses for large construction and infrastructure projects. Towards the end of my time doing that work, there was a push towards 'early contractor involvement' (ECI), otherwise known as collaborative contracting. The main idea of ECI is that the contractor who will be *delivering* the project should be involved in the *design* phase.

The idea is to refine scope, iron out potential problems early and spot opportunities for innovation. The value is often immediate, with the grand plans of architects and designers quickly grounded by the rapid assessment of a contractor, who says extremely useful things like 'You can't put a pipe there' or 'We don't have the equipment for that'.

Systems improvement is similar. When we try to drive change, we tend to split up the 'design' and 'construction' phases by tier. Like big infrastructure projects, keeping these phases separate is risky. We underestimate the scope of change, get people offside and make silly mistakes.

No system should be designed in isolation or without the input of the people who work inside it, benefit from it or need to use it. If that involves customers, then you need their voices in the room. It doesn't need to be via complicated user testing but it must include a conversation. Bringing internal teams, users, people managers and subject matter experts into the room when you're still in the planning phase is critical.

Like ECI, however, this requires good planning in advance so that you have the time to do these conversations well – plus a genuine openness and commitment to considering different views and changing tack if required.

How can you bring internal teams and customers into your strategic conversations?

FIX THE SIEVE FIRST

When we find a weak link, it's tempting to immediately invest in additional resources. However, throwing more money at a sluggish system by hiring more people or investing in new technology without changing how it works is like pouring water into a sieve.

Consider a small council struggling to keep up with a surge in resource consents, thanks to multiple subdivision developments kicking off at once (a change in the external environment). The regulatory manager is insistent – he needs more staff, fast. The chief executive and council are inclined to agree. They're fielding phone calls from irate developers, delays are making headlines in the local newspaper and there's an election coming.

Before approving additional recruitment, we need to take some other critical steps:

- *Optimise the way that bit works.* Find ways to make the existing point of failure stronger. If planners are taking longer than expected to assess applications, first pay attention to how they're managing their time, documents and calendar, to ensure they're operating at optimum capacity. We might need to change the policy around flexible work to accommodate variable schedules or eliminate unnecessary steps in the existing process.
- *Subordinate everything else to serve that bit.* This step can be a tough pill for high-performing teams to swallow. It means taking the parts and relationships that are connected to the problem child and directing their energy in support of the slowest stage.

For consent processing delays, that might mean redirecting staff who currently handle online applications to redesign the form, ask additional questions of applicants or present supporting information in a fashion that's easier to work through.

- *Bring in extra resources.* Only when you've worked through the first two steps should you consider adding additional staff or investing in a new tool or technology. Even then, you should start with the minimum viable investment. For consent processing, this might mean bringing in two contracting staff to manage the overflow or upgrading the software plan used to process applications.

How can you take a closer look at your weakest link? Can you optimise or change it before you throw more resources at it?

THINK DOLPHINS, NOT WHALES

How much time does email save you?

I know, it's laughable. The average professional spends almost a third of their workday reading and answering email, according to one McKinsey analysis. We're not seeing the payoffs that smarter technology and 'time saving' software, email and other systems promise. 'Productivity-enhancing technologies' often just make knowledge workers' jobs more complicated.

Videoconferencing was heralded as the next workplace revolution – thanks to the reduction in commuting, we could all be working fewer hours per day. The reality looks quite different. As teams shifted to work-from-home arrangements during the COVID-19 pandemic lockdown, I watched people take their existing back-to-back meeting schedules and jam them into Zoom. It was different, sure. We no longer had time to think as we walked between meeting rooms, and struggled to find time to pee!

The reality is that new systems and technology tend to create jobs, not reduce them. Be very wary of adding anything new. There should be a high threshold for adoption. Where possible, adopt the classic wardrobe rule: one piece in requires one piece out.

Most importantly, every process should be the minimum viable version of itself, requiring the least amount of resource, complexity and support possible. Overcooking a process in the name of quality or transparency is easy to do – but like all defaults, can be hard to rewind once in place. When designing systems, start with the minimum and add with care.

What is the smallest step you can take to improve the weakest link in your process?

What we've learned so far

- We need to dissolve problems, not solve them.
- Systems aren't what we buy or do, but how we work.
- We need the right people involved.
- We should zoom out visually and messily.
- We should zoom in carefully and change the smallest thing possible.

Your next step

Create a visual map of the System in your world - your team, organisation, sector or community - and talk about it with others. What are you missing? What is the weakest link?

LESSON 11

Put your money where your mouth is

I once worked in a council that attempted to rebrand. *Attempted*, because the process was never completed. After extensive consultation on a new logo, management decided on a soft launch to help people with the transition. The new logo wasn't widely appreciated, so without the requirement to use it, many teams preferred to use the old branding.

The results were disastrous. Letters, leaflets and advertisements were being distributed by different departments with different branding, and the new vehicles looked nothing like the existing fleet. There was rampant disregard for the direction of senior management, some of whom quietly endorsed the behaviour of their staff. It was a shambles.

This persisted for years, until a new communications manager came in, took charge and secured support for a non-optional rollout of the new brand across the business. Within weeks, the old branding came off the doors, vehicles went to the sign-writers, old letterhead was recycled and a policy and style guide was adopted by the executive team, requiring all staff to comply with the new regulations.

Systems leadership means *making the new way the only way* and holding people accountable for their behaviour. If you need to transition or run two systems at once, be diligent about setting a deadline for the old system's demise and communicate that well in advance.

Given a chance to hold onto the old, there will always be people that do. Communication and engagement are critical, as is support, training and resourcing. But without strong leadership, true systems change will never get off the ground.

Consider requiring visible evidence of uptake. If you've just instituted a new customer request management system, ask for weekly reports on the numbers. If you've rebranded, randomly audit communication before it leaves the door. If you've instituted new document management infrastructure, refuse to reply to emails with attachments instead of links.

As a last resort, introduce penalties for non-compliance. If your sales team members are resistant to their new pipeline system, only pay commission on sales with accurate data entry.

How can you make the new way the only way?

SYSTEMS CHANGE ISN'T FREE

But systems change needs more than just leadership – it needs resourcing.

When we roll out new software, we should allocate 10 to 15 per cent of our budget to promotion, training and support. Despite this, I consistently see teams expecting to absorb this cost and time into existing roles and budgets. The results are consistent: slow uptake, errors and frustrated staff.

Get expert advice at the beginning about the size of the job, and budget more time and money than you expect; odds are you'll need it.

This isn't something that you can do after the fact; implementation resources need to be allocated at the beginning of the project. No new system should launch without the training, support and information to make it usable from day one.

Be creative! Think about scheduling live demonstrations, showcases or roleplays. Make online recordings, case studies and materials available. Allocate one team member as a 'roving support person' who answers questions on the spot for the first month. Free people to shadow those who are already adept in the new system. Appoint mentors and change champions. Make it as easy as possible to do the right thing.

Are you investing enough in resourcing and support? How easy it is to do the right thing?

WAIT A MINUTE

In one organisation I work with, we've had to start referring to particular restructures by their month as well as their year, because there have been too many changes in the last three years to know which one we're referring to. Senior managers are plotting their next 'realignment' as I write this book, seemingly oblivious to the erosion of trust and performance in their teams. Surely this one will do the trick, right? Unfortunately, they're unlikely to find out, before there's another reshuffle at the top table and a new senior leader feels compelled to make their mark with another operating model shift.

This kind of churn is expensive, time-consuming, exhausting for staff, and a one-way ticket to cynicism and mistrust. Valuable institutional knowledge – some of which takes years to regain – gets lost, and unforeseen difficulties and gaps derail progress.

As leaders, we generally don't give things enough time to work before changing them again. Our new system barely has the chance to start producing the expected results, yet we feel pressured to try something new. We restructure, and before people get their heads around their new responsibilities and reporting, leaders get nervous at a temporary drop in performance, or a dip in results on their engagement survey, and start moving things around again.

It's a self-perpetuating cycle. When we don't adequately invest in change, or give it a chance to work, we create a black hole of value – one we attempt to fill with yet another change to fix the last poorly implemented system. Real systems change requires brave leadership to set a reasonable, expected timeframe for onboarding and transition, and the courage to give something long enough to stick.

Are you giving things enough time to bed in?

KEEP TWEAKING

Life is a continuous beta-test. While we need to give things time to stick, it's also true that systems change is never a one-and-done thing. Remember: today's adaptations are tomorrow's default. Even the best-designed system or process will need to shift and evolve in response to its environment.

Your options for continuous improvement systems are dizzying – an entire cottage industry has sprung up around the term, as the demand for agile methodologies skyrockets.

One of the earliest versions, a system change standard, is the infamous Plan, Do, Check, Act (PCDA) cycle. Other teams I work with prefer the less formal Gemba walk method, where leaders are required to get out of their offices regularly and 'walk' the front line, interacting with staff on location.

One of my favourite clients is a council in rural Australia, where Peter, the general manager, makes a point of taking regular out-of-office wanders. In a chance encounter with a groundsman at a council-owned cemetery recently, he stopped for a chat to see how the landscaping was going. When the groundsman suggested the council lease an adjacent empty paddock for grazing – 'it'd save me a heap of work and make us a bit of money!' – Peter took action immediately. The value of the data he collects on those wanders has sparked process improvements in everything from plant maintenance to payroll – and generally only takes a few minutes' chat.

Toyota is a darling in the manufacturing world and renowned for its Kaizen culture of continuous improvement. Toyota runs 'katas' which set regular challenges for staff, who are encouraged to find ways to improve their daily routines and supported with discussion groups. Katas, practised regularly, create a default of incremental change that keeps the entire organisation moving forward.

Whatever system you choose to use, a process for regular review and continuous improvement should be built into every team or organisation. It doesn't need to be complicated – in smaller teams, having a running shared document or a regular meeting that encourages people to contribute their everyday frustrations can often be enough to head off potential issues early, before they become a headache.

Are you keeping an eye on things? Do people have the real opportunity to tweak systems as you go? How could you make that happen?

CHECK YOUR SYSTEMS

How do you know if your systems are any good? Try assessing them against the following criteria:

- Safety
- Simplicity
- Sustainability.

Safety

In 2018, the world watched the fallout from the first fatal accident involving a driverless car and a pedestrian in Arizona, the US. People took to the airwaves to voice their concerns and fears, unallayed by repeated assurances from the auto industry about the safety of the new technology. Policymakers listened. While driverless cars were initially expected to be widely available by 2020, the timeline has come and gone without significant legislative progress.

The irony is strong. Driverless cars are anticipated to significantly reduce incidents and fatalities on our roads, saving many lives. Putting aside bigger debates about whether investing in vehicle technology is the right call for cities that should be focusing on active transport and pedestrian connections, current evidence supports serious investment in self-driving technologies. The debate strikes right to the heart of systems change: people are nervous about giving up control, preferring to rely on 'people power' despite stacks of evidence about the unreliability of human reactions.

People are unreliable. We're easily distracted, we forget things and we frequently make mistakes. Good systems are reliable and accurate – in fact, they're far more reliable than people. They mitigate risk by making quality and accuracy more likely. Done well, systems save us from ourselves and improve the consistency and quality of our results. Good systems are designed to promote accuracy and safety through quality control, assurance and review.

Do your systems improve the quality of your outcomes?

Simplicity

Nothing excites me more than an unexpectedly easy customer service encounter. It's better than Christmas. I experienced this recently when I moved to a new house and changed utility providers. Expecting problems and delays, I was thrilled when the changeover was quick and painless.

The Global Simplicity Index tells us that simplicity pays. The majority of consumers will spend more for an effortless customer experience and straightforward value offering.

Aldi regularly tops the index. Compared to other supermarkets, Aldi carries fewer options per product category. It has a more consistent store layout across locations and a crystal-clear customer promise that is consistently delivered on – affordable, quality products. Simple brands, like Aldi, Google, Netflix and Ikea, understand that making an experience easy is one of the most powerful ways to make customers happy.

You might not be surprised to learn that most organisations are not so simple – or that the public sector takes the cake for complexity. The average government agency is 30 per cent more complex than some of the world's largest companies. From the customer's perspective, this means that service can be needlessly complicated. Internally, this means that policies, processes, strategy and organisational design act as handbrakes to progress.

Simplicity is the ultimate sophistication.

Leonardo da Vinci

We add complexity and bureaucracy out of fear. Simplicity would require bravery, clarity, risk and trade-offs. Ironically, this complexity erodes the very trust we are trying to protect. The bigger we get, the worse we seem to be, creating a tyranny of scale that amplifies complexity with duplication, overlap and inefficiency.

Our customers aren't the only ones getting frustrated by this – staff suffer, too. Engagement and productivity are the obvious victims, but the more insidious stifling effect of needless complexity is risk aversion. When people stop sticking their necks out because it doesn't feel worth trying to change anything, the quality of our service suffers.

Our problems are complex, but our organisations shouldn't be. Get a better handle on your business by making the invisible obvious and stripping out the unnecessary. What's right is generally what works.

Do your systems remove unnecessary steps and make work easier?

Sustainability

The natural environment cannot accommodate more industrial growth. Our natural resources are being extracted and disposed of faster than they can be renewed. Nowhere is this more evident than with fossil fuels. The more we remove, the more that ends up in our air, water and landfills as carbon emissions, or by-products and waste. Despite this, our economic model depends on continued growth to work – requiring an ever-increasing amount of extraction and production to sustain the population.

Our organisations often work in a similar way. Set up to depend on the efforts of people, continued growth and success require increasing input of time and labour. In other words, more staff, working more hours, doing more things. Like the natural environment, this weakens our structures over time, creating burnout through over-extraction.

Good systems reduce our dependence on people by simplifying, automating or streamlining processes so that we can do the same, or more, without putting more pressure on our resources. When we delegate to our systems, we begin to establish a more sustainable way of operating.

Do your systems reduce dependence on people?

What we've learned so far

- Systems change needs leadership, resourcing and support.
- We need to give things a chance to bed in before we change them again.
- Systems change is an everyday job – we should always be tweaking.
- Good systems are safe, simple and sustainable.

Your next step

Consider how you can make the right way the only way.

SYSTEMS

What we've learned

If you really want to escape the things that harass you, what you're needing is not to be in a different place but to be a different person.

Lucius Annaeus Seneca

A strong systems leader never takes anything at face value. Asking bigger, better questions every time you're faced with an issue becomes instinctive over time.

While your colleagues might panic every time something doesn't go to plan or an old issue comes up yet again, it's different for you. As a systems leader, you have the gift of seeing the bigger picture and understanding how it all fits together. Take comfort in the knowledge that people are rarely stupid or evil – just doing their best in an environment that doesn't always make it easy.

Don't get bogged down with what's in front of you. Finding the energy to put your head above the parapet isn't always easy, but what's right rarely is.

Here are a few attributes of hero versus systems leaders:

Hero leaders	Systems leaders
Blame people	Blame process
Uphold convention	Challenge defaults
Solve problems	Dissolve problems
Guess	Ask people
Buy systems	Build systems

What you can do

The first step to taking a systems view is to apply some self-awareness. How are you complicit in maintaining the status quo, even when it's not working? You are always part of the system you seek to change. Part of what makes systems so tenacious is our deeply held and unhelpful tendency to cling to what feels comfortable.

Understanding systems requires absolute flexibility – awareness of how things fit together; agency to change your environment (rather than people); resilience to keep trying, adapting and evolving.

Systems are about continuous movement. As soon as you have your part or process nailed, something in your environment will shift. Like most things that matter, systems are never one-and-done – they're dynamic and need to be adaptive. Remember: yesterday's adaptations are today's routines.

When you're confronted with a frustration or an inefficiency, dig deeper. Ask 'why' a few more times. Dig for the original source of the crime.

Test relationships and workflows. Get in the habit of drawing swirling systems diagrams instead of process charts. Ask the people who have to use your systems what's working, and what isn't.

When you're tempted to hire more people, or buy a new thing, pause. Fix the sieve before you pour more water into it, by understanding how everything fits together. Ask challenging questions. Bring people on board.

Above all: always assume positive intent. If people aren't doing the right thing, it either isn't the easiest option, or it isn't the right thing.

Three key questions

1. Why are they doing this?
2. So, what can we change?
3. Is it really, though?

MODULE 4

PERFORMANCE

For when you need to make things happen

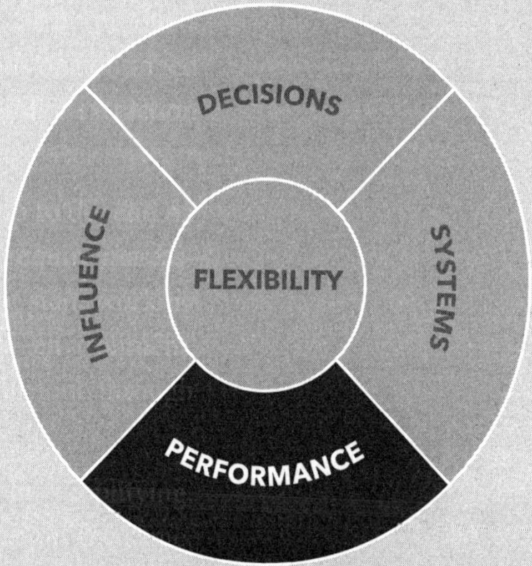

LESSONS IN THIS MODULE

12. We're all imposters
13. Campervans are everywhere
14. This game isn't for amateurs

LESSON 12

We're all imposters

Do you find yourself guiltily logging in, checking emails and chasing things up when you're supposed to be off the clock? Do you feel like you're the only one who can't get on top of this stuff? What is everyone else doing that makes it look so easy?

Here's the truth: everyone is overwhelmed. Everyone is managing details they feel should be out of their remit. Everyone is struggling to know where to start.

Like most invisible issues, we're making the problem worse by not acknowledging it. When we feel like everyone else has their act together, and we're the only ones who can't keep up, we don't talk about it – forgoing the opportunity to do better.

There's a huge disconnect between these two things:

1. An epidemic of overly operational senior leaders
2. Widespread operational performance failure across all sectors, in all organisations of all sizes.

We're staggeringly over-optimistic about what we can deliver, by what time, at what cost. Two-thirds of public sector projects are late, over budget or don't deliver on their expectations. Seventy per cent of corporate business change programmes fail. Despite teams experimenting with everything from project management to agile methodologies, the success ratio of projects hasn't increased in more than 20 years. Whatever we're focusing on right now isn't working.

In their book *Leadership on the Line* Heifetz and Linsky use the metaphor of the dance floor and the balcony to describe the balance we need to strike between achieving perspective and intervention where it counts. The authors ask us to imagine we're dancing in a large ballroom, focused on our partner and our dance moves. When we're asked to recall our experience, we would describe the band, the enthusiasm of the other dancers and the vibe on the dance floor. The view from the balcony, however, might have been quite different, as we saw the empty sections of the floor, or how the crowd responded to different songs and genres.

We can't be in both places at once. We need the perspective of the balcony to make good decisions, but when it's time to make change we need get back on the floor.

We've spent the first three modules of this book getting you up on the balcony, where the perspective is clearest. But when it comes to performance, we need action: it's time to get back on the dance floor.

However! This module comes with big, red, loud, bold, capitalised, underlined, neon lights warning:

> ***Not all activity is created equal.***

Greg McKeown talks about the *paradox of leadership:* the further you are promoted, the further you move away from how you perceive you add value. This can lead to newly promoted senior leaders hanging onto their old responsibilities while trying to take on new ones. You know the type – they have a team of clever people, but they're working every night because they don't have enough time for the 'real work' now, and nobody else can do it right. This kind of behaviour really sucks. It's a terrible use of energy, and the quality of their work is rarely as good as they think it is. Everyone loses – teams are disempowered and hamstrung, and leaders feel like harried, unappreciated victims.

I once worked with a council where a second-tier manager was reading and signing off every land information memorandum (LIM) report before it left the building. These reports, which contain the property information people need before they buy a house, can run into hundreds of pages and are usually handled by an intermediate planning or building advisor. When challenged, he was defensive: if the report was inaccurate, council could be liable! The possibility of a mistake was a huge risk that he couldn't let go of.

But the outcome of hanging on so tightly was toxic: hundreds of hours, every year, dedicated to a job that should have been completed three tiers down. The fear of losing control or making a mistake created a bottleneck that hamstrung the planning, regulatory and customer service teams, slowed down the turnaround time on reports and stopped him from being able to focus on the more valuable aspects of his job. He was operating way below his paygrade, and everyone suffered.

The most successful leaders know better than this. They're scrupulous about how they allocate their time, attention and investment. They intimately understand their value and what drives performance in their teams. Connected to results that matter, they strike the right balance between support and accountability for those responsible for making things happen.

Signs you need to tune into performance

- You're not getting shit done.
- Your team makes stupid mistakes.
- You feel unfocused and hurried.
- You're busier than ever, but not making meaningful progress.

THE THREE Cs OF PERFORMANCE

Drawing on the actionable strategy model from my first book, *From Strategy to Action: A Guide to Getting Shit Done in The Public Sector*, performance is about three critical components:

1. *Clarity* – A clear sense of purpose that identifies where we need to focus and what success looks like.
2. *Coherence* – Total alignment in the way we work and how we manage time, energy and resources.
3. *Commitment* – Consistency, quality and accountability for performance.

Neglect any of these three, and you're making life harder than it has to be.

BE CLEAR ON WHAT MATTERS

I see so many leaders plan upside down. They fill their calendar and programmes, then work out how they'll measure success. It becomes a self-perpetuating cycle, where they get tangled up in justifying activity by framing it well, rather than holding themselves accountable to their goals.

Performance leaders do things differently – they begin with the end in mind. When we work that way, target results drive our decisions, rather than the other way around. When we're crystal clear on what we're aiming for, we organise our lives and establish projects accordingly.

Remember the PayPal story? PayPal made a splash in 2016 when it pulled the pin on a new office building in North Carolina, after learning about the transphobic policies staff would have to follow. PayPal's clarity about creating a world without violence, hatred, intolerance or discrimination enabled it to make strong, clear decisions about what it should do when faced with a trade-off.

Interestingly, PayPal is also an incredibly high-performing organisation. While it doesn't often get the same attention as Apple, Amazon or Google, its stock performance rivals all three.

Dan Schulman, PayPal's president and CEO, credits that performance to the clarity of the company's mission. In a 2016 quarterly results report, he wrote, 'We have a clear mission at PayPal. We want to democratize financial services and become an everyday, essential service for underserved consumers'.

His number one tip for being a leader? Clarity of vision and intent. That focus guides the company's internal decisions as well as product launches and partnerships. The launch of 'PayPal Gives' in 2015 encouraged its global workforce to embark on 'missions' that improve sustainability and social outcomes in and outside of the company. The absolute focus on doing the right thing shows up across the board, and employees love it. People are engaged, retention rates are well above the industry average and innovation is thriving across the business.

There is nothing so useless as doing efficiently
that which should not be done at all.

Peter Drucker

This kind of leadership is rare and powerful. Only 10 per cent of all leaders fall in the 'purposeful' category, but these are the magic ones who inspire their teams to greatness. When people have something to care about and connect to, as well as the autonomy and empowerment they need to make it happen, they are more than twice as productive as a satisfied employee. Purpose pays.

What is the true purpose of your team or organisation? Are you clear on that? How are you making that a reality?

FOCUS ON THE INTERMEDIATE

While purpose is useful, performance isn't about nebulous, high-level goals. It's about driving results. When I was a policy analyst, our well-intentioned template for making policy recommendations included a section on strategic alignment. The idea was to provide a sense-check, to make sure we were making decisions that lined up with the big picture. The reality was an effort in justification. In all my time writing and approving recommendations, I never found a project that couldn't be made to fit a hazy outcome like 'a thriving community'.

End outcomes, or benefits, are about long-term aspiration. What are you trying to make happen? They have inherent lag and ambiguity, and tend to say things like 'a connected community' or 'a sustainable future'. These outcomes are critical for strategic decision-making, but when we try to link them with daily activities they lose their meaning quickly. To close the gap, we need to focus on *intermediate* outcomes that we can be held accountable for, and that act as a tangible lever to our big-picture or end outcomes. For a connected community, for example, we might focus on volunteer engagement, or participation in neighbourhood events.

Do you know what really makes the difference in your team or organisation?

Performance: a case study

At a large university I worked with, the board and executive team needed student bums on seats to remain financially sustainable. Preliminary research had identified the initial student experience as a key driver of financial performance across their sector, and information on hand supported that too.

The data was clear: if enrolment was fast and easy, we could attract more students, retain current students and reduce wasted time internally. So off we set to put together a programme of work.

While conversion, retention and internal productivity might have been our big-picture end benefits, these goals weren't particularly useful for department heads who needed to lift the performance in their teams. To get everyone focused and on board, we needed to understand what would *drive* those big-picture benefits. Knowing we wanted to convert more potential students, we had to dig a bit deeper to uncover the links that convinced students to come and to stay. Those were our intermediate drivers - and included things like certainty about fees, more intuitive programme planning, faster turnaround on enrolment offers and easier scholarship applications. We mapped it all out, and the figure on the next page shows what we came up with.

In most teams it's a best guess. With our university, we used qualitative data from across the education sector, as well as internal data around customer insights and time management, to dig deep. Using reliable and accurate information, and testing that with focus groups and internal observation, we were able to interrogate the things that shifted the dial on attracting, converting and retaining students, as well as understand where we were currently wasting the most time.

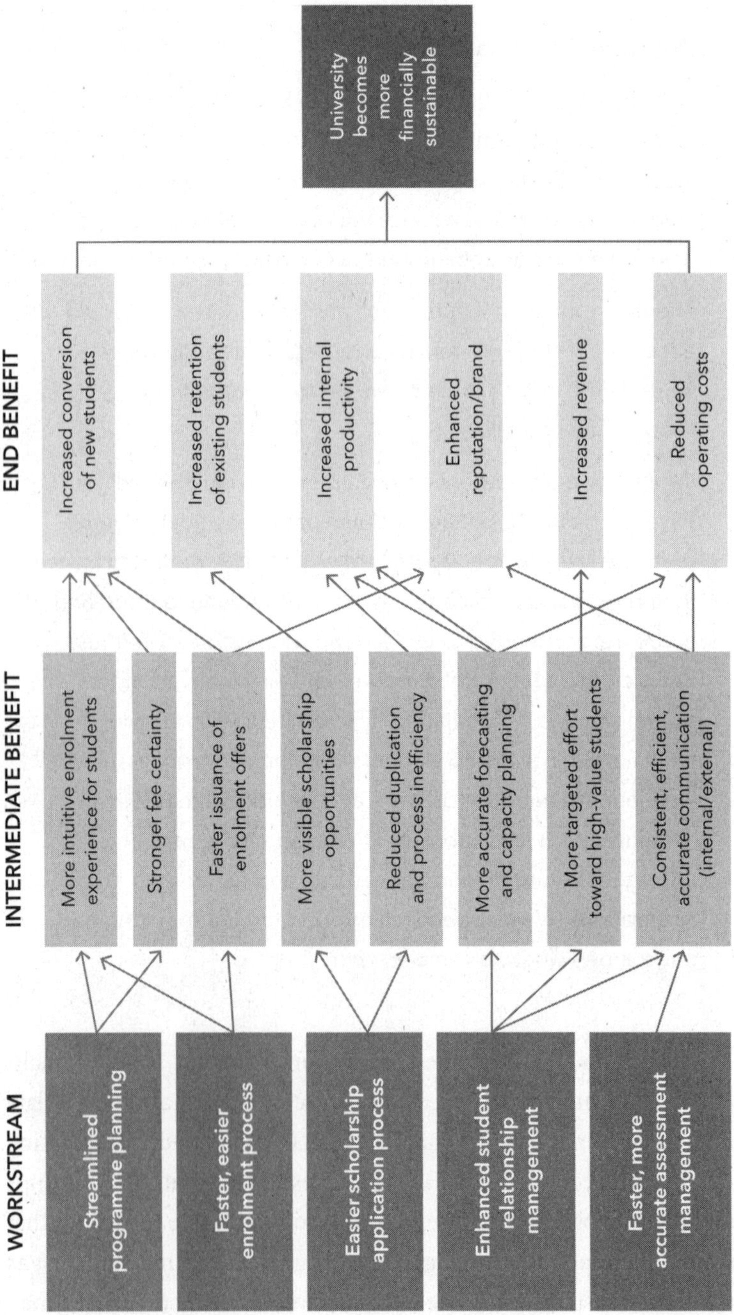
WORKSTREAM
Streamlined programme planning
Faster, easier enrolment process
Easier scholarship application process
Enhanced student relationship management
Faster, more accurate assessment management
INTERMEDIATE BENEFIT
More intuitive enrolment experience for students
Stronger fee certainty
Faster issuance of enrolment offers
More visible scholarship opportunities
Reduced duplication and process inefficiency
More accurate forecasting and capacity planning
More targeted effort toward high-value students
Consistent, efficient, accurate communication (internal/external)
END BENEFIT
Increased conversion of new students
Increased retention of existing students
Increased internal productivity
Enhanced reputation/brand
Increased revenue
Reduced operating costs
University becomes more financially sustainable

Investing in the factors that drive quality and profitability requires mapping the topology of our team or organisation, to work out which factors drive performance. Will we get the most value out of training our people or investing in technology? Should we improve recruitment or focus on customer service quality?

Unfortunately, there's no easy answer. It depends on big-picture things (your industry) and individual factors (your organisational history or the personalities of people on your team). In software and banking, customer loyalty is a more important determinant of profit than any other factor. In these industries, a 5 per cent increase in customer loyalty can increase profits by 25 to 85 per cent. Understanding the impact shifts make is enormous. At Xerox, for example, shifting customers from 'satisfied' to 'very satisfied' makes an incredible difference: the 'very satisfied' customers are six times more likely to repurchase equipment than those who are 'satisfied'.

In other industries, employee loyalty is considered the strongest determinant of success. Virgin chief executive Richard Branson famously claimed that at his airline, customers come second to employee welfare.

Our university came to understand that initial student experience was the key driver behind big-picture performance. Students were far less likely to switch institutions once enrolled in an academic programme. So, making the enrolment experience easy and enjoyable was the biggest direct driver of revenue. Making that happen depended mainly on backroom systems and internal performance.

Finding the drivers can be tricky. The key is to gather evidence that doesn't rely on personal opinion. Everyone has their own idea about what will make things work – one manager will make the case that a new website is the performance panacea, while another has been harping on about email inbox limits in every meeting for the last three years. But those assumptions are usually off.

Rhian Silvestro, renowned academic on performance, suggests using a 'performance topology' approach to finding out which links apply to your team. 'Performance topology' is a fancy name for doing what we did with our university – working backwards from your most important objectives, figuring out the links and measuring correlations against the various things you do to shift the dial. There's no substitute for hard work, which usually means sifting through information to make sense – or simply starting from scratch and experimenting.

So, before you spend up large on a customer request system, work through information on hand to test how much impact dissatisfied clients have on your bottom line. Before you send your analysts on productivity training, establish a baseline for how well they use time now, and measure it again three months later. Take the time to map your topology and commit to using that information to get smarter about what drives performance.

No information is perfect. But if we don't test those links and assumptions against reality, we're committing to burying our heads in the sand. Like policy reports, anything can be justified – but that's not enough to make a compelling case for investment or intervention.

What information could you review to work out the performance topology of your team or organisation? What makes the most difference to the results you deliver?

CHECK IF IT WORKS

You won't know if you've picked the right drivers unless you check. So, set the parameters up early. What does success look like? While this seems like a simple question, performance measurement is also one of the most poorly understood and least useful components of most organisations.

That's not a dig at well-meaning analysts or leaders, but a reflection of how decision-making information has been corrupted and turned into a stick to beat each other with. Most issues stem from *what* we measure, and *when* we set it up. Performance measurement should be considered at the very beginning, guided by our target outcomes, and grounded in sound, relevant information that is useful for making decisions.

The university we worked with was able to focus on the tangible measures that stemmed from intermediate outcomes. Because we knew what success looked like in the short-to-medium term, performance measures were able to deal specifically with things like how long the enrolment process took, how many clicks were needed to get to the end of an application, how satisfied students were with the speed and ease of scholarship applications, and how long staff spent correcting duplication and inefficiencies.

Statistics are like bikinis. What they reveal is suggestive, but what they conceal is vital.

Aaron Levenstein

When we start looking at intermediate outcomes, it's easy to get hung up worrying only about the things that are easy to measure. That puts the blinders on our perspective. Performance leadership is about more than measuring widgets or keeping an eye on the bottom line. Instead, it thinks about the long term and asks tricky questions about what we're *not* seeing.

In his book *Upstream: How to Solve Problems Before They Happen*, Dan Heath tells the Expedia call centre story. In 2012, Expedia was analysing the performance of its call centre. On the face of it, things were going well. The call centre was efficient and provided excellent customer service. Reps were well trained and resolved customer queries quickly, reducing the time spent on calls, increasing throughput and progressively reducing the cost per call. On the face of it, this was a performance success story… right?

A look at the bigger picture changed everything. Head of customer experience, Ryan O'Neill, decided to zoom out and interrogate the call centre data differently. In doing so, he was shocked to learn that 58 per cent of customers who booked online placed a call for extra help. How could this be possible? A look at the data revealed the answer: most customers were calling for a copy of their itinerary. In 2012, 20 million calls were logged for that reason alone. At $5 per call, itinerary requests represented a $100 million haemorrhage on Expedia's balance sheet. The problem, of course, didn't lie within the call centre itself. Quality control weaknesses in the online form and a high volume of Expedia emails going to spam were compromising the online process, so people weren't receiving their itineraries as expected.

After pulling together a team from across the business, simple changes were made, including self-service itinerary downloads and changes to the email system. In rapid time, the proportion of customers calling for support – for any issue – plummeted from 58 per cent to 15 per cent, due in no small part to the elimination of almost 20 million support calls.

This story is a brilliant example of what can happen when everyone is busy performing well at their job – but *only* their job. Bigger-picture problems, which rest slightly outside of our department or silo, are easily missed. When it's no-one's job to optimise the whole, the parts don't work. Truly effective performance leaders do both – optimise their part, and ensure they ask bigger, trickier questions about what drives those trends in the first place.

For you, these will look different, but, as a rule, you need to choose measures that:

- Focus on outcomes
- Reflect the big picture
- Are useful for making decisions.

GET OVER ATTRIBUTION

Good measurement focuses on outcomes – the meaningful things that shifted because of our effort, not the things we did. But outcomes are subject to forces outside of our control, and if our measures are used as a tool for punishment or reward, we get understandably nervous about taking responsibility for outcomes.

What if our students are dissatisfied by enrolments because of the courses on offer, rather than the experience provided throughout enrolment? What if staff aren't slow because of the tools at their disposal, but because they haven't been trained correctly?

Ultimately, unless we're making a meaningful shift at the end, our efforts are for nothing. Unless we can be comfortable with a spectrum of attribution, and the impact of things outside of our control, we won't really know if we're making a difference.

When you're trying to lose weight, what's the most important indicator? Is it the number on the scale? Or the way your jeans fit? Better yet: how healthy you are, and how confident you feel?

Performance leaders don't measure performance to prove a point, or to look good. We measure performance to get decision-making information about what's changed.

Test your performance measures – how many are about what you *do*, and how many are about what you've *changed*?

PICK A STORY SUITE

No single measure or number can tell us everything we need to know.

We should measure a collection of things that, together, indicate whether the change is heading in the right direction. The key word here is *change*, which means measuring trends in context. An 80 per cent customer satisfaction rating means nothing unless we can answer questions like: Is this an increase or a decrease from previous levels? What is the 30-day trend? What about the 12-month or five-year trend? Which customers are most satisfied, and which least? Does this correlate to changes in service quality or speed? How much does it cost us to shift satisfaction by one or 20 points? What did we change recently that could have contributed?

Select three to five measures that, on their own, might not give you everything you need, but together are a good indicator of whether things are trending in the right direction.

MAKE MEASURES USEFUL

Good performance management gives useful information that feeds into sound decisions. If we were having a beer at a BBQ and I asked you how your new initiative was going, what information would you draw on to answer my question? Whatever that is – that's the useful stuff you should be measuring.

You might find yourself telling me a story or giving me an example – and that's great. Meaningful performance measurement should be about more than targets and indicators. Use rich information like case studies and stories to build engagement, show success, capture good and bad news, share lessons learned and change culture. In our *What's on Your Mind?* podcast, we keep an eye on viewer counts, shares and comments, but some of the most useful and valuable feedback comes via the messages from listeners, as they share how our thoughts and ideas have changed the way they think or encouraged them to try something new.

Do you use your measures in conversation or meetings to check in on how things are going? How can you bring stories into your performance measurement?

What we've learned so far

- We're all imposters.
- Purpose drives performance.
- Intermediate benefits drive performance.
- Make measures meaningful to check if things are working.

Your next step

Map the intermediate drivers of performance for your team or organisation and test them.

LESSON 13

Campervans are everywhere

My grandparents have been talking about buying a campervan for years. The topic comes up every couple of months, and recently, they've been close. There's always a brochure lying around, a tab or two open on the laptop and regular trips to expos and dealers. Despite that, there's still no campervan in their driveway. While the dream of setting off for a few months each year still holds water, the rest of their lives doesn't quite align yet. They've got ongoing commitments at home, businesses to run, children and grandchildren to look after and animals to feed.

Most people have a metaphorical campervan in their lives. Mine is martial arts. I loved karate as a kid, and as an adult, I often think how much I'd like to take it up again. I follow a few different clubs on Facebook, check out training timetables every six months and fantasise about how enjoyable it would be to train and compete. Unfortunately, like my grandparents' campervan dream, the rest of my life doesn't lend itself well to my goal. Running around after kids and their activities, along with a busy travel schedule, means that committing to a club and regular training just doesn't work.

In both cases, the drive is there – but the alignment isn't. Our goals and lives aren't in coherence, which stops us from making any progress. If I were serious about making martial arts a priority, I'd change the way I work and live. We often substitute talk for action, but we don't align our work and lives. The stuff we really want or need to do becomes a metaphorical campervan. It pops up regularly in meetings and preliminary investigations play out, but the sacrifices and changes necessary to make it work seem too large.

Real performance needs something to shift: the goal or the way we work. In truly coherent people and organisations there is absolute alignment between what is wanted and the actions to get there. In the PayPal example, there is alignment between what the company says, what it stands for, how it spends its money and how employees are supported to live those values.

Alignment is another easy buzzword – but how do you do it? You need to:

- Set clear priorities
- Live your priorities
- Control your attention
- Manage risk.

SET CLEAR PRIORITIES

Stop trying to do everything at once and learn to focus your energy. In a 2010 study, Harvard psychologists Matthew Killingsworth and Daniel Gilbert found that people spend almost half of their waking hours thinking about something other than what they're currently doing. Half! And it's costing us.

Multitasking is a myth. We can't do two things that require high-level brain function at once. What we *can* do is task switch. When we do that rapidly, it feels like we're multitasking, but we're losing time and energy between jobs and reducing the effectiveness of both. You might think you can talk on the phone and write an email at the same time, but given the interference between those tasks, you're definitely selling at least one, and probably both, communications short.

Attempts to multitask can lead us to take up to 40 per cent longer to finish a job than if we'd just focused on one thing intently at a time. We're juggling (and ball dropping!) and it's dangerous: not only do things take longer, but we miss things – typos, contextual clues and the chance to save something to memory.

This is bad enough at a personal level, but when we're multitasking at an organisational level, the results can be catastrophic. When organisations inadvertently overload themselves with too many projects, productivity plummets, quality suffers and employees burn out. It happens far too easily. With every business unit launching their own well-intentioned initiatives, the project count adds up quickly.

My internal alarm bell rang loudly when the chief executive of a small agency I was working with proudly told me they had more than 100 critical projects on the go… this year. It's shocking, but at least this CEO was aware of how many demands he had of his staff. Many are not. Senior leaders are prone to 'impact blindness', where they simply don't see the cumulative demand on their teams to deliver and support projects across the business. Even when we can see all the plates we've got spinning, it's easy to underestimate the cross-functional impact each one has on everybody else.

This often happens when we don't have an exit strategy. Because it's tricky to get something funded or approved in the first place, many leaders are reluctant to let things die – even when they're past their use-by date. Government is particularly bad at this, thanks to a 'use it or lose it' funding mentality. It's time to cut the load, and let things go.

Take multitasking off your - and your team's - agenda. Commit to regularly reviewing the cumulative load and how it all fits together.

LIVE YOUR PRIORITIES

Early in my career, one of my jobs was to write and project-manage an annual plan. Every year was the same story – going through each budget with governance, line-by-line, only to get to the end, tally up all the ad-hoc decisions we'd made and find that they led to a budget increase we didn't like. So we'd go and slash, trying to find some 'tricks' to get it over the line (plundering a quiet reserve, messing about with depreciation, seeing what could be deferred or capitalised). The trade-offs were bitsy, opportunistic and not at all strategic.

Worst of all, it was generally a far cry from the idealism of the planning sessions we'd held only a few weeks earlier, where we'd boldly set goals and outcomes for the coming year.

Never ask anyone for their opinion,
forecast, or recommendation. Just ask them what
they have – or don't have – in their portfolio.

Nassim Nicholas Taleb

We take a similar approach to how we spend time – first we fill it up, then we try to slash things around the edges without making hard decisions. We end up with a complete disconnect between what we say matters and what we do. Coherence requires some tough calls. When I work with overcommitted teams and leaders, I often ask: 'Who are you going to choose to let down today?'. If you accept you'll have to let people down either way, it makes sense to do so respectfully and ahead of time – rather than at the last minute when they are counting on you.

When it comes to priorities, we need to walk the talk. The way we choose to spend and invest our time, money and energy should align directly with the priorities and direction we set in our strategy, put on posters or claim in team meetings. This is walking the talk with a price tag.

Aligning with your priorities means changing the way you schedule and spend your time and making visible, consistent commitments to others that reinforce your focus. Total alignment requires you to make it real, let people down and treat your calendar as the most precious resource you have available.

What would your ideal day look like? Your ideal week? How would you spend your time and energy if you had no constraints? What activities would you be focusing on that would lead to the most valuable contribution? Start from there, rather than tweaking at the edges.

Getting to the next level always requires ending something, leaving it behind, and moving on. Growth itself demands that we move on. Without the ability to end things, people stay stuck, never becoming who they are meant to be, never accomplishing all that their talents and abilities should afford them.

Henry Cloud

When I move house, I get to engage in my favourite activity: throwing things away. Every time, I sort through all our stuff and become merciless with what qualifies for box status. No danger of hoarding around here!

If just reading about me throwing away my stuff makes your heart beat a little faster, you're not alone. It's hard to get rid of things we already have – even when we know they're not serving us, or there's a better option out there.

I hear the same protests all the time. 'I have to do everything I'm doing!' 'Nothing is negotiable!' I call bullshit. Strategic leaders know that real change can't be *as well as.* We're already at maximum capacity. Real change needs to be *instead of.*

And sure, that's fine if we're releasing things we don't enjoy, don't add value or we don't care about – like my boxes of stuff when I move. Those are choices between right and wrong. How about when we need to choose between right and right? Or chuck out stuff we're still using? This is uncomfortable territory. But if we can't let go of the good, we don't grow.

In *Necessary Endings*, Dr Henry Cloud uses the beautiful, poignant metaphor of a rose bush, which always produces more life than it can sustain. That puts the onus on the gardener to carefully cultivate this life, enabling the bush to reach its full potential. Directing enough nourishment and energy to the great buds requires culling the poor performers.

This is true for the existing buds, and for new buds that arrive, too. It's hard to acknowledge that some need pruning. It's even harder to remove new ones before they've had the opportunity to grow.

But the alternative is to keep piling on and watch a potential future suffer. Everything you say 'yes' to comes with an opportunity cost. This cost might be resources, your time and attention, or ultimately your health or values.

You'll have to prioritise every day. Every. Single. Day. If you're doing work that matters, you'll have to let things go, let people down and make tricky trade-offs regularly. There is no one-and-done. Instead of agonising, make peace with that. Seize your agency in communicating it and get used to the discomfort.

What do you need to let go of? What buds could you prune?

CONTROL YOUR ATTENTION

Attention is the taking possession by the mind,
in clear and vivid form, of one out of what may seem
several simultaneously possible objects or trains of thought.
It implies withdrawal from some things in order to
deal effectively with others.

William James

I was gifted with a shoulder injury recently, which forced me to become very careful about how I spent my time and energy. I tired quickly, had limited use of my right arm and could no longer put in the same number of hours as before. I had to ask tricky questions such as: 'What are the things that only I can do?', 'How do I add the most value?', and 'What can I take off my plate, with some training or investment?'.

The answers were telling – I was doing lots of things I didn't need to. When I looked at how I usually spent my week, I realised there was administration, communication, client work, design and online updates that could be handled by other people in my team, or by automating the process. The beauty of that realisation with my arm in a sling and reduced capacity was that I wasn't looking for opportunities to fit in *more*. Instead, I was trying to find space to do *less*. What I didn't anticipate was how useful and transformative that space would be for the creative and strategic work I never seemed to have time for. When I came back on deck, I found myself with new ideas, spotting new opportunities and thinking differently about how we add value to our clients.

Performance isn't about quantity; it's about quality. While incapacitated, I started to think of my time and energy as less of a stew, and more of a jus – the distilled, concentrated value-adding impact that adds the finishing touch. Even better, I built more sustainability into my practice – so that things would work, even when I couldn't.

Finding new ways to be more productive is a serious modern challenge – for economies, organisations and people. When it comes to ourselves and our teams, we get confused about productivity, conflating it with efficiency or output. The truth is productivity has little to do with efficiency and everything to do with value. Real productivity isn't about doing things quickly; it's about getting more out of what we've got. The norm in most teams and organisations is still for people to view time and impact as linear – more time or people would create a greater impact. But you had more time, you'd just waste more time. Productivity is about how we spend our time, not how much we have.

What's your comparative advantage - the thing that you do better than anyone? How much time do you spend on that thing? How can you spend more on it?

MANAGE RISK

Firefighters have a demanding job. They do all the stuff we expect in a crisis – like turning up and fighting a roaring blaze and making decisions in the moment. Behind the scenes is the important work we don't see – getting prepared for the next big fire and working to create conditions that lessen fire's ability to take hold. Move up a level on the strategic ladder and it gets even more interesting – some fires are left to burn, and others still are purposely ignited.

The Australian bushfires of 2019 were a case study in performance leadership. With too many burning to fight them all, some had to be left to burn. Even more important were the intentional, controlled burns lit ahead of time to mitigate the blazing fires.

Managing risk is the same. Part of the job is responding to issues as they present, while another is front-footing fires before they can kindle. The ability to manage in a crisis is as much to do with the prework as it is disaster response.

We need to set the world on fire occasionally, too, by thinking big and embracing new opportunities. Sometimes, brave leadership means thinking like a bush firefighter and setting a controlled burn to clear out the underfoot so we can move forward.

When we manage risk well, we're not focused on the nitty-gritty. We don't know the entries in our health and safety register and couldn't tell you what's on page 47 of the business continuity plan. Performance leaders manage *strategic* risk by preparing for the worst.

Operational risk, which we tend to know a lot more about, asks the question: 'How do we keep everything ticking over?' Strategic risk asks: 'What might stand in the way of meaningful change?' When thinking about our job like this, we think bigger and refocus decision-makers on the stuff that matters, managing for outcomes and uncertainty.

At the operational level, we categorise events by calculating their probability and multiplying it by their potential impact. At the strategic level, the focus shifts from *events* to *categories* and from *mitigation* to *readiness*. The questions you're asking are not 'What is most likely?' but rather 'What's the worst thing that could happen?' The things that throw us off course – disaster, pandemic, financial crisis – are not the things we easily see coming. In an uncertain and complex world, we can't be expected to know what might be coming next, but we should be prepared to manage through disaster.

I often run an exercise with executive teams, politicians and boards called 'It's Been A Disaster!' We work through a hypothetical scenario to answer one key question: what are the absolute *worst* things that could happen in the next year? We fill the board with everything from staff issues and PR nightmares all the way through to natural disasters and financial crises (or, y'know, pandemics). Once we've got everything on the board, we talk about how we could prepare, and how we might respond. Most importantly, we acknowledge that at least a few of those things are likely to happen, in some version

– and we don't know which ones! The value of this exercise isn't just our appreciation for the inevitability of disaster, but for our agreement on how we'll stay the course confidently when things *do* go to custard – because they will.

I ran this exercise with a local authority before COVID-19. After staff identified their most catastrophic risks, they agreed ahead of time on their response and what they needed to prepare. (The table opposite shows their action plan.) When COVID-19 struck, this council hit the papers for leaning towards a conservative fiscal response – slashing spending, freezing staff numbers and capping rates! Not what they'd decided at all. I quickly sent them the table opposite as a reminder of what they'd discussed in peace times. My message: 'You knew this might happen and decided in advance to spend your way out of it. You've done the preparation. Don't back out now'.

Performance leadership isn't about eliminating risk – that isn't possible. Your job is to be ready to respond when the worst does eventually happen, and to have the confidence to pull it off.

What are the most significant risks you face? How would you respond? How could you prepare?

Most significant risks	Response	Readiness
Economic fallout (major industry fails or leaves, tourism loss, financial crisis)	Spend (stimulus and investment)	Leave debt buffer Proactive investment in local communities Establish alternative funding streams Strong local and national relationships
Critical infrastructure failure or deficit (natural disaster, unplanned failure)		
Sudden population shift (migration, demography)		
Large funding shortfall (central government cutbacks, tourism loss, major project blowout)		
Compliance failure (regulation change, environmental disaster, negligence)		

What we've learned so far

- Campervans are everywhere.
- Be clear on your priorities, and align your life to suit.
- Your attention is your most valuable resource.
- Strategic leaders manage for uncertainty.

Your next step

Design your ideal day, or week, and consider what might have to shift to make that possible.

LESSON 14

This game isn't for amateurs

The Last Dance was one of 2020's biggest Netflix hits. Documenting the heyday of the Chicago Bulls, it focused on Michael Jordan's career. Nobody does commitment quite like Michael Jordan. Every day, on or off season, Michael Jordan worked out. Every day, he shot baskets. When the team spent their afternoons ahead of a game relaxing, Michael was out on the golf course strengthening his complementary muscles. He was at the arena at least two hours before every game, impeccably dressed in a suit and tie. Win or lose, Michael showed up every day and demanded the best of himself and the people around him. Michael Jordan is no amateur – he's an indisputable professional.

In *Turning Pro,* Steven Pressfield makes the distinction between the two. While the amateur is tangled up in distraction, convention and validation, the professional is prepared and committed to mastering technique and enduring adversity. The amateur lives in the past or the future, while the professional is here, in the present, taking action.

Doing the right thing isn't always easy, and doing the easy thing isn't always right. Professionals don't expect it to be. The difference between performance leaders and the rest is not that they have less to deal with. It isn't that they don't fail, either. Every leader faces change, uncertainty, distraction and failure. Every leader is busy. But professionals keep showing up.

> *I've missed more than 9000 shots in my career. I've lost almost 300 games. 26 times, I've been trusted to take the game-winning shot and missed. I've failed over and over and over again in my life. And that is why I succeed.*
>
> Michael Jordan

To be a professional requires commitment. You need to:

- Take ownership
- Set bottom lines
- Walk the floor
- Respond well in a crisis.

OWN IT

How many of you work with someone who endlessly complains about a lack of time, but they're always on the operational frontline 'fighting fires'? Maybe you are that person?

At General Motors, the dress code consists of only two words: 'Dress appropriately'. When asked about the policy, GM's chief executive, Mary Barra, said:

> *You really need to make sure your managers are empowered – because if they cannot handle 'dress appropriately', what other decisions can they handle? And I realised that often, if you have a lot of overly prescriptive policies and procedures, people will live down to them.*

Taking ownership isn't about doing everything yourself. For those of you leading a team, ownership is about owning the outcome – and delegating the work. Effective delegation is about so much more than handing over responsibility, too. Good delegation gives people the autonomy to make decisions, responsibility for the outcome and the resources and support to make it possible. In short: effective delegation is about *empowerment* and *accountability*.

If you don't trust the people you lead to deliver, nothing gets done without you. Empowerment sounds fluffy, but it's about much more than gushy appreciation and pithy slogans. Empowerment doesn't mean a hospital pass; it requires *enablement* to work. We get far better results when the emphasis shifts from how to get more out of people to how to invest in them so they're motivated and enabled to do a good job.

Empowerment goes beyond permission. It means providing meaningful support through training, mentorship, regular communication, opportunities to advance, profiling success and showing recognition by spreading it. Make it easy for people to do a good job and they probably will.

How can you make it easy for people to do a good job?

One of my mentees, let's call her Kate, is a third-tier manager in a large government agency. The epitome of a supportive leader, she invests real energy and empathy into coaching and developing her team, making sure they have what they need to do great work. Kate's always thinking about how to get the best out of her people and makes a concerted effort to help them grow. In a recent Leadership Versatility Index (LVI) 360-degree assessment, her team attested to what a supportive and encouraging leader she is, and how much they appreciate her style.

Kate is also incredibly focused on delivery. Her team members know they're expected to deliver the goods, and that deadlines matter.

When it comes to setting expectations around quality and deadlines, she's clear – even borderline forceful at times. Despite all of this, Kate scored consistently poorly in one critical area, across her team, boss, peers and colleagues: *accountability*. She was baffled. How could that be true? How could she be an empowering, delegating leader, with clear standards… and rate so poorly?

This is a common trap for committed leaders. Kate is great at ownership – when it comes to her own behaviour. But successful delegation isn't about how you hand over tasks or empower others; it's how you respond *when things go wrong*. It's easy to delegate when things go to plan. But if you get speed wobbles when things go off track and jump in to save the day (like Kate often did), you undo much of that good work.

Holding people accountable by setting boundaries and allowing them to experience the consequences of their behaviour isn't manipulative or selfish. The reality is, when you insist on saving the day, you're usually more worried about protecting yourself, or your reputation. Leaders that take ownership don't throw people under the bus, but they also don't set up a victim-and-saver dynamic by shielding people from consequences. Stop robbing others of their growth.

How can you allow people to experience the consequences of their behaviour?

SET BOTTOM LINES

In 2019 I worked with senior executives in the community sector to build performance leadership. We used role-playing exercises to practise communicating clear expectations, and it was genuinely surprising to discover that many people found it difficult to say things like, 'Here's what we need you to do' and 'These are my expectations of you'. More telling was the reaction of others in the room, reflected in statements like 'I felt safe' and 'I appreciated the clarity'. In this organisation, facilitative leadership (where leaders are encouraged to be supportive, hands-off and avoid being too directive) was so strongly valued it came at the cost of clear expectations and meaningful support for outcomes. It was a classic case of strengths overused.

In times of urgency, uncertainty or compliance, facilitative leadership can be damaging. Not only because it provokes further unease, but because it can be disingenuous. Over the past 20 years, leaders have been encouraged to consult and engage with their teams and communities over policy and direction. This has been mostly positive – except when it hasn't. People aren't stupid. They know when you are 'consulting' for compliance rather than participation. And your teams are the same.

Performance leadership strikes the right balance between facilitative and directive leadership by knowing when to tell. A performance leader gives meaningful direction by:

- Setting clear goals and expectations ('In this company, we put customer service first.')
- Being open with information ('Our current average response time to customer queries is 36 hours because we're spending too much time chasing other departments for information.')
- Operating within a set of defined 'bottom lines' and behaviours ('We will respond to all customer queries within 24 hours.')
- Carefully defining roles and responsibilities ('I will lead the difficult conversations with the rest of the executive team. The customer service lead is responsible for daily monitoring and developing better information-retrieval processes. All customer service representatives are responsible for meeting their target times and asking for support when required to make that possible.')
- Balancing autonomy and accountability ('You will be supported to make the changes necessary to deliver on our target. If you

need new resources or systems, speak up. I'll consider all proposals and suggestions.')

- Monitoring helpfully by checking in, rather than checking up. ('How are you finding the new target times? What help do you need to make it easier?')

There are some things that you can't compromise on – and, too often, those things aren't clear to the people involved until they fail. If you've never stipulated the response time ('people just know that's the rule!'), then you can't expect people to comply. No-one should have to read your mind.

Set clear bottom lines ahead of time, communicate them clearly and stick to them... but be careful. Quality standards are a gateway drug to perfectionism. Bottom lines are not about getting carried away or doing *everything* well. We should draw a line in the sand for our most critical performance drivers – whether that's internal service quality, customer experience or advertising – and make it possible to achieve those standards.

Real professionals are comfortable with 'good enough' in the areas that don't add the most value, because they focus time, energy and attention where it makes the most difference.

Typos and grammatical errors are a good example. While you should *never* let a typo slip through in your marketing collateral, the same mistake in an email is unlikely to be a problem. Errors in board reports, social media posts and policy recommendations sit somewhere in the middle – not great, but unlikely to affect the final result.

If you accept that not everything will be done perfectly – because it won't – the value comes from seizing agency over what you're willing to let slide, so that you can make sure the things that really matter are less likely to be compromised.

Are you clear about what people need to do, and to what standard? Do you know what you're willing to compromise on - and what you're not?

WALK THE FLOOR

In the show *Undercover Boss*, a senior executive or company owner goes 'undercover' in the lower tiers of their company for a week. Viewers feel smug as the out-of-touch leader goes on a journey of realisation, reconnecting with customers and frontline staff and gaining a deeper appreciation for how real people live and the impact of decisions made in the boardroom.

Like most reality television, *Undercover Boss* leaves a lot to be desired. The outcomes are predictable, and the focus on being heart-warming leads to decisions that annoy my systems-focused brain. (If you've realised that your minimum-wage workers are struggling to have secure housing, don't buy one employee a house – pay them all a proper wage!)

However, the overarching lesson is useful. Leaders at all levels need to stay connected to the purpose, meaning and impact of the work the organisation does. When you're rushing from one meeting to another, signing off reports and fielding emails, it's easy to forget why you're doing it, and how significant an impact your decisions have on people's daily lives.

As a freshly minted policy advisor at a little council in provincial New Zealand, my desk always sported a copy of Michael Mintrom's *People Skills for Policy Analysts*. My biggest takeaway from that book was something I wasn't taught at university or mandated to do in my job: get out of the office. Whenever you're working on a project, reviewing the effectiveness of a policy or decision or trying to understand something new, Mintrom implores, you need to close your internet browser and get your hands dirty. This elementary yet eye-opening advice totally changed the way I thought about my work. Years of working with public leaders have only reinforced my position on this. Anyone making decisions that impact the lives of others – in business, government or elsewhere – has a responsibility to appreciate what their decision-making means.

Connection means getting out of the daily grind and seeing the big picture. Stop second-guessing your middle managers' decisions or proofreading your team's reports and stand alongside them in the field occasionally. We can't carry out site visits or go undercover every week, but we should keep that connection alive. Speak with stakeholders regularly, spend time with your frontline staff and make a point of getting out of the office.

Include the voice of your frontline, stakeholders, beneficiaries and customers when you make decisions about what matters. Implement a strong customer feedback loop, so you have your finger on the pulse of what people value. Use frontline workers' insights to interpret that information and make meaningful improvements. Make it OK to raise problems – create a precedent where people know that their ideas and concerns are taken seriously. Schedule exit interviews with customers and employees. Listen. Take them seriously. Walk a mile in others' shoes; without a real understanding, you're unlikely to make the right call.

How can you 'walk the floor' and connect with outcomes more regularly?

RESPOND QUICKLY TO CRISIS

New Zealand, be calm, be kind, stay at home.

Jacinda Ardern

Performance leaders don't *react* in a crisis – they *respond*. Remember, the reactive leader is often driven by the fear of losing control and the fear of failing. Strategic leaders don't share these fears. They tap into their agency to make good decisions, and then get moving at the first sign of trouble.

On Tuesday 11 August 2020, New Zealand saw the end of a remarkable 102 days without community transmission of the coronavirus. At 2.30 pm, the first positive result was returned. At 2.40 pm, the head of the Northern Region District Health Boards notified the Director-General of Health. Within 15 minutes, health officials were meeting to discuss the situation. The Prime Minister, leaving a public appearance, was told an hour later and headed directly to Parliament to meet with an all-of-government response group and the Ministry of Health, convene a group of government ministers and make swift decisions – all in accordance with government response protocols. Shortly after 9 pm, the Prime Minister and Director-General of Health fronted a press conference, announcing the resurgence and placing Auckland into alert level three lockdown, and the rest of the country into alert level two, for 72 hours, while further information was gathered and testing carried out.

The government's response was incredible – swift, clear and calm. New Zealand's government has become an international case study in crisis leadership, and the August resurgence is just one example of this leadership in action. When it comes to New Zealand's COVID-19 response, there are some obvious and early lessons that apply to all performance leaders faced with responding to a crisis.

Do you react in a crisis? Or do you respond?

To be a professional requires rapid response. Doing this well requires you to:

- Be clear about your *intention*
- Use expert *information*
- Seek genuine *inclusion*

- Communicate with *incision*
- Demonstrate *integrity*.

Intention

The speed of the 11 August response would not have been possible without the work that had gone into developing pandemic response plans well before the COVID-19 outbreak, commitment to a shared goal and a clear framework for response. New Zealand made its goals clear in the earliest stages of the pandemic – to eliminate the virus. While other administrations fumbled around deciding whether to try to suppress the virus or simply mitigate the effects, swayed by dissenting voices and pressure from across their communities, the Ardern government was unequivocal: *we will eliminate the virus*. While this stance has not been without contention, it has undoubtedly been clear. That clarity of purpose has paid dividends, enabling the preparation of focused, effective response plans, clear messaging to the community and absolute alignment across all levels of government.

How can you prepare ahead of time for crisis, so you can respond better when it hits?

Information

Performance leaders aren't controlled by fear; they're guided by facts. New Zealand's response to the coronavirus pandemic has been led by the latest scientific advice and evidence at every stage and a *willingness to follow that advice*, even when the consequences aren't popular. The landmark Imperial College report, released on 16 March 2020, represented a combined effort of infectious disease experts across the globe. The findings were clear: failing to respond would be catastrophic; epidemic suppression is the only viable strategy, and action would need to be swift to be effective. The report shaped the thinking of many administrations across the world, but not all were brave enough to act.

Gathering facts quickly and acting on the advice of experts has been instrumental in the success of New Zealand's COVID-19 response. For all crisis leaders, the willingness to be led by expertise isn't just good leadership – it's a smart way to overcome our fears, biases and hubris.

Do you value expert information? Does your team trust data?

Inclusion

Performance leaders don't just call on experts; they bring together different perspectives to tap into a bigger, better brain. While information provides us with conceptual *depth*, inclusion offers conceptual *distance.*

Intellectual conformity is dangerous. In *Rebel Ideas*, Matthew Syed talks about the CIA's failed detection of 9/11 to demonstrate the dangers of homogenous thinking. The CIA's failure to spot the attack can be partially attributed to the lack of diversity and inclusion in their ranks. Pre-2011, the CIA analyst workforce was overwhelmingly white, Protestant and middle-class, recruited from a small selection of schools and universities. This lack of diversity created a huge collective blind spot. Not only did the CIA not *have* diversity, it didn't *value* it, either. The organisational narrative, over decades, was that diversity would mean sacrificing excellence for political correctness. This severely constrained the variety of conceptual frameworks, background knowledge and worldviews available to their analysts. Diversity wasn't a compromise, it was critical – and they failed.

In a crisis, we need a strong collective effort to respond effectively. The COVID-19 response is the perfect example – for physical distancing and home lockdowns to work, people need to comply. Mobilising that collective effort requires diverse input and perspectives. In New Zealand, this meant inviting stakeholders from across the spectrum into the conversation and considering more than just work and the economy. It meant thinking about people's wellbeing, how different cultures and family structures would be impacted, and what kind of mental health support was needed to keep people safe and happy amid uncertainty.

When a crisis hits, resist the temptation to barrel forward alone; otherwise you risk overlooking essential elements of the problem and ignoring wider implications and consequences. Reach out and involve others – you can't serve others if you don't understand them.

Do you include the right people in your decisions? What new relationships might you need to build?

Incision

The most studied aspect of Jacinda Ardern's coronavirus leadership has been her communication style. Ardern's balanced deployment of exactness and emotion has connected and resonated with her 'team of five million', delivering unprecedented public approval ratings of over 80 per cent and compliance rates of more than 90 per cent.

Strategic leaders know that for the people they lead and serve, fast, frequent and imperfect information is better than not knowing. They know their communication is not about them, how they look or what people think of them. It needs to be:

- *Fast:* When everything turns to custard, false information and rumours spread faster than any virus. When people's jobs are on the line, this is doubly true.
- *Frequent:* Update people as often as necessary, preferably at a regular cadence they can come to count on. In New Zealand, the daily COVID-19 press conference became an institution in many people's calendars.
- *Clear:* When ambiguity is rife, there's no room for uncertainty in your message. Crisis leadership is a time to tell – which means precise instruction in simple language.

- *Real:* In uncertain times, people need to connect – and if they can't connect to you, they won't connect to your message. Be human.

How can you bring these communication principles into your crisis leadership?

Integrity

If people don't believe you, they can't hear what you're saying.

In 2011, a FedEx employee got into hot water after he was caught on film throwing a computer monitor over someone's fence. The video was soon uploaded to YouTube and has since racked up 10 million views. Within two days, FedEx publicly apologised, made no excuses and shared its plan for correcting the issue. The response was shared by video and in a blog post, and came directly from senior executive Matthew Thornton – humanising the message. The effectiveness of this response wasn't just in its speed but in its action and transparency. Going further than just promises, FedEx shared details about the employee's future and also revealed that the video would be used as an in-house training resource to stop similar issues from happening again.

Good performance leadership is about more than honesty – it's about transparency, and immediate, meaningful action. Don't hide.

How can you make sure your response is transparent and honest?

What we've learned so far

- Performance is not for amateurs.
- Professionals show commitment through ownership, quality standards, connection to outcomes and crisis response.

Your next step

Consider which aspects of your work need a bottom line… and which don't.

PERFORMANCE

CHEAT SHEET

What we've learned

The picture we have in our minds of the high-performance leader is mostly a caricature. They're busy, fast-paced, authoritative and assertive. They're hard. They work harder, push harder and try harder. This caricature is a highly visible, totally inaccurate meme.

Any one of us can be a high-performance leader, but the things that underpin this are less visible than we might think. The performance leader is calm, focused and empathetic. They're clear on what really matters, carefully align their work and life to suit, and they're diligent about turning up, even – no, *especially* – when it's hard. It's a tricky balance. Most of us lean too far one way or the other – getting our hands dirty too often and undermining our teams' autonomy and growth, or being too hands-off to drive quality and accountability. There's no such thing as perfection, but we should be aware and mindful of our balance at all times.

Here are a few attributes of pedantic versus performance leaders:

Pedantic leaders	**Performance leaders**
Try to do everything	Only do what matters
Set unachievable goals	Align their life and work
Panic under pressure	Keep showing up
Plan for the best	Prepare for the worst
Micromanage	Set bottom lines
Save the day	Hold others accountable
Panic under pressure	Respond quickly and calmly

Leaders who drive real performance are focused professionals. They commit. They apply absolute rigour in their planning, prioritisation and quality control – and they're also totally accepting of inevitable disaster, disruption and change. They know what to zoom in on, and what to step back from. They recognise when to support and enable, how to build accountability, and when to respond and amend. Performance leaders know when to be on the balcony and when to get on the dance floor - and, most importantly, how to find the intermediate link.

At its core, performance leadership isn't about working harder than anyone else - it's about clarity on where we focus, coherence in how we align our effort and commitment to quality and accountability.

What you can do

Review this performance checklist to see where you could improve your current leadership:

- ☐ Get the basics right.
- ☐ Set clear goals.
- ☐ Focus on what adds the most value.
- ☐ Simplify, automate or delete everything else.
- ☐ Commit religiously.
- ☐ Focus on ensuring quality and managing risk.
- ☐ Delegate with meaningful autonomy and hold people accountable.
- ☐ Act quickly when things turn to custard.
- ☐ Rinse and repeat.

Take a close look at what really drives meaningful outcomes in your life, team or organisation. What are the common themes? What has the most impact?

Map those drivers against the results you're looking for and use them to set bottom lines. For your personal life, that might be core habits, like exercise, diet or sleep. For work, it might be customer experience, response times or internal relationships.

CHEAT SHEET

Take the time to consider your priorities – what matters most to you? What do you most need to focus on to do the work that really matters? Consider the work you're focusing on that is out of alignment with those priorities, design your ideal day or week and then take action to prune some of the buds that are getting in the way of your success.

Remember: campervans are everywhere. If you're not committed to a goal, stop beating yourself up about it, decide which balls you're willing to drop, and let it go.

Stop treating disaster like an unexpected event and start preparing for inevitable change. You might not be able to predict what's coming, but you can change your mindset and work on readiness for challenge.

This game isn't for amateurs, so take some space to consider your commitment and professionalism. Are you really dedicated to your cause? Are you living your values? If you aren't, something might need to shift: the goal, or your behaviour.

Most importantly, breathe. Regularly take the space to get clear on your focus and priorities, and keep tweaking. Performance leadership is an everyday job. Like meditation, don't judge yourself when your mind wanders – accept that it's part of the process, and keep coming back.

You've got this.

Three key questions

1. What does 'good' look like?
2. Where should we focus?
3. How will I hold myself, and others, to account?

MODULE 5

INFLUENCE

For when you need to mobilise others

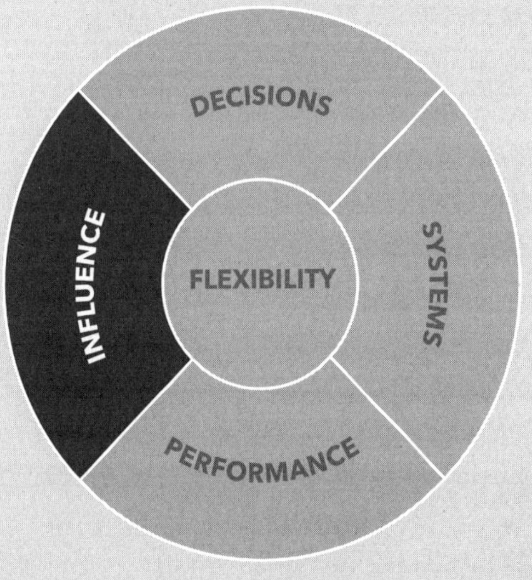

LESSONS IN THIS MODULE

15. Leaders need followers
16. Nurture your network

LESSON 15

Leaders need followers

Influencer marketing is the most popular guerrilla marketing strategy of the last 10 years. In 2018, more than 80 per cent of marketers reported that using influencers was working. And it was, generating twice as many sales as paid ads.

The first wave of influencer marketing was all about celebrity endorsement – Kim Kardashian reportedly earns more than half a million per Instagram post! – but this is starting to shift. Large-scale influencer marketing is on the decline. Micro-influencers, though – those closest to their target audience – are bucking that trend, as businesses start to value credibility and deep engagement more than reach and quantity.

Micro-influencers (word of mouth on steroids) are now delivering the best results for brands, with more engagement, more clicks and a higher return on investment. One study found that influencers with just 1000 followers generated 85 per cent higher engagement than those with 100,000. While those with large follower counts get more 'likes', micro-influencers get more meaningful comments, sales, traffic and competition entries. They're more credible, more impactful and generate better results.

But what *is* an influencer? An influencer is a person whose opinion is trusted and sought after, with the power to affect others' decisions and a reputation for knowledge and expertise on a particular topic that they use to share content and ideas.

Leadership is about influence. Nothing else.

John Maxwell

Influence is not always about who has the biggest following. Anyone can be an influencer if they're trusted and respected by the people they need to reach.

In most workplaces, just 3 per cent of people currently drive 90 per cent of the conversations. Those super 3 per cent people have more impact, leverage and visibility and are far more likely to make meaningful progress in their work.

Interestingly though, having real influence doesn't mean you win everyone over. Even the most challenging transformations, such as revolutions and regime changes, only require active participation from 3.5 per cent of the population. Erica Chenoweth, a political scientist at Harvard University, completed a longitudinal study of non-violent civil disobedience. She looked at movements including the 1986 People Power movement in the Philippines, the Singing Revolution in Estonia in the late 1980s and the Rose Revolution in Georgia in early 2003, finding no campaigns failed after achieving 3.5 per cent participation. You don't need everyone – just the critical few who make things happen.

We might not have Instagram engagement metrics to prove our efforts, but we're all influencers in some capacity. Even the most introverted person will influence 10,000 others in an average lifetime. If you're a senior leader and include the impact of your decisions on your team, customers, citizens and wider organisation, that number easily grows to hundreds of thousands.

Strategic leaders are influencers. What we do with that influence is up to us.

ALL CHANGE IS PEOPLE CHANGE

He aha te mea nui o tea o?
He tangata, he tangata, he tangata.

(What is the most important thing in the world?
It is people, it is people, it is people.)

Māori proverb

It doesn't matter how clever you are or how good your idea is; without support, change dies or doesn't ignite at all. If you want things to be different, you need the people who do stuff, make decisions or form part of your operating context to change what they're doing.

In *Lead the Room: Communicate a Message that Counts in Moments that Matter*, leadership communication expert Shane Hatton explains this clearly. With communication, we get engagement, and with connection, we get trust. But with influence: we drive change.

People want to be part of something bigger, but talk about change is often met with exhaustion. Change is constant, and many of us are tired of it. We're burnt out and suspicious of the next new thing that promises the world, when the last thing was such a poorly implemented disappointment. We are sceptical about new distractions and interruptions to an already full workday and generally resent adopting new tools if we can't see clear benefits. The bar for engagement is high, and we're generally not doing enough to get people on board.

Just 5 per cent of leaders succeed at changing behaviour, and those leaders spend as much as *half* their time thinking about and actively influencing others. Half!

Whether we're trying to bring in new ideas, new technology or new operating models, we rarely invest enough attention and resources into creating the behaviour change necessary to make business change successful. Trying to make things happen without putting the time into human behaviour is a fast-track to frustration. Strategic leaders work a bit harder.

Signs you need to build your influence

- Your work isn't getting the attention that it should.
- You're not getting traction with important projects.
- You'd like to manage difficult stakeholders more effectively.

Influence is not about your content; it's about your connection. Because people are inherently social (though it doesn't always feel like it), we crave the opportunity to be part of something bigger with others. While some schools and workplaces go to great lengths to minimise social 'distractions', this kind of counterintuitive policy shuts down a powerful part of our brain and a shared connection that can be harnessed for learning, productivity and wellbeing.

I often meet leaders with an attitude of 'I don't go to work to make friends'. I get that, I really do. One of the reasons I've never lasted in an employment environment is the obligatory niceties. Why am I signing a leaving card for someone I've never met? How could they possibly value my clichéd contribution? Why should I contribute to a morning tea for Jane's baby? I can't stand Jane, and I've got work to do.

Cultivating influence doesn't mean you need to join the social club, but it does mean that you need to be personable and connect with people on a real level. In my case, I've bypassed the social club approach to instead cultivate individual and personal connections with treasured clients, sharing a regular text or message or glass of wine to celebrate success, commiserate failure or simply chew the fat. Some of my oldest clients are now dear friends.

Good relationships don't happen by accident. Influence won't fall into your lap. Like lifelong friendships, connection to our children and fulfilling romantic relationships, these connections don't just happen. They require us to understand others deeply, to have compassion for differences and manage conflicts. Most importantly, they need intentional care, and a commitment of planned time and energy, or they wither and die.

How can you make the time and space to nurture your relationships?

I recently ran a coaching session on influence with a group of transport policy analysts who were having trouble with a collaborative strategy process. The goal was to reduce city-wide emissions, and the plan on how to do so had to be agreed to across multiple tiers of government, in alignment with business and community groups. It wasn't going well. Stakeholders were dropping like flies. Trust was bottoming out, and even getting people to meetings was becoming a struggle.

So what wasn't working? Three key things:

1. The person leading the project had only recently bought in to the importance of the work. Before this, they'd just been trying to get it done.
2. The goal of the process centred around developing a document, rather than how it would be used and implemented by all partners to the process.
3. The work was controlled tightly by the project lead with little opportunity for others to contribute to bringing it to life.

Influence is about intent, impact and inspiration (and this particular strategy process was missing all three):

- *Intent* is about you… kind of. It's about your motivation and commitment to serve others. Leaders don't care about getting credit; they care about change.
- *Impact* is about them – the change that you need others to make. Unless we've changed people's behaviour, we haven't had influence.
- *Inspiration* is about creating something bigger than you, or them. When we create a movement, develop a partnership or build a tribe, our ideas take on a life of their own.

IT STARTS WITH YOU

The first few minutes of any meeting or job interview are funny, aren't they? All that small talk about the weather, kids or sports… why do we do it?

Simple really: to be more likeable. When you're likeable, people seek out every bit of competency you've got to offer. People buy from, hire, work with, take to the airport early in the morning, coffee with, and marry people that they *like*. You don't need to be the best-looking, the most charismatic, the highest performer or the most popular. But being likeable is a shortcut to influence that gives us some margin and permission, removing the pressure for perfect work or ideas.

Leaders who rank low on likeability are quickly written off: they have a one in 2000 chance of being regarded as effective, according to research published in *Harvard Business Review*. Not flash. Once people like you, though, they're much more forgiving. It's harder to be an asshole to your friends.

Being likeable isn't just for attractive extroverts – it's about attunement. In *The Likeability Factor*, Tim Sanders describes it as 'increasing your capacity to deliver emotional benefits to others'. Sanders argues that you can boost your 'L-factor' by enhancing:

- *Friendliness:* your ability to communicate liking and openness to others
- *Relevance:* your capacity to connect with others' interests, wants and needs
- *Empathy:* your ability to recognise, acknowledge and experience other people's feelings
- *Realness:* the integrity that stands behind your likeability and guarantees its authenticity.

Likeability is about finding common ground. We like people who are like us and have similar backgrounds, beliefs, interests and personal styles because they reaffirm our validity. Once we're familiar with someone, we're more accepting of their differences, and can skip the initial stuff and get straight to work.

How can you find more common ground with your team, colleagues and stakeholders?

WALK THE TALK

Waste no more time arguing what a good man should be. Be one.

Marcus Aurelius

Credibility is everything. Like the celebrity influencers who've had their moment in the Instagram sun, movements without trust and substance at their heart don't last. In the long run, your integrity, consistency and reliability will be what you're remembered for – not the short-term results you had to cut corners on to deliver.

The level of influence you have on others is directly proportionate to the level of trust they have in you, and trust is a prize worth having. Teams with high trust produce better results using fewer resources. Leaders with high trust enjoy the benefit of the doubt every time they enter a new room, have a new idea or approach a new client, customer or employee. Their reputation precedes them – and carefully nurturing that should be a high priority for any strategic leader.

In the consulting world, it's often said that you're only as good as your last job. As a leader, the principle is the same. Your word is everything, and if you lose integrity with your peers, teams or stakeholders by not doing what you say you will, your long-term credibility and reputation will be compromised.

You need the trust of your teams to be an effective leader, and more broadly, your organisation needs the credibility of its customers, public and community for the license to operate. Living your values is hard for a reason – but it's the only long-term strategy that works.

What are you doing to build trust?

BE VISIBLE

Visible leadership is like parenting – your kids learn a lot more by watching what you do than listening to what you say. Just as businesses value goodwill as an intangible asset, leaders need to value their reputation and integrity.

I often work with organisations that have lofty goals but don't live their values. One of my clients, a local council, was intent on promoting its 'recruitment brand' – encouraging people to move to its community and take up hard-to-fill technical roles. Job ads touted the benefits of living in such a family-friendly place, promising a break from traffic and city pressure. The problem came when we looked a layer deeper – they didn't even have a flexible working policy! Employees aren't stupid. They know when what you say and what you do are different things, and they behave accordingly.

Visible leadership involves encouraging and modelling momentum – bringing your ideas and values to life and sustaining their existence. Practise what you preach and be what you ask of others, because everything falls to bits when there's an inconsistency.

Are you practising what you preach?

CONNECT WITH INTENT

When I speak at conferences, I often confuse organisers with my lack of slides. I hate them. They're good for pictures, and practically nothing else.

When we confuse influence with talking people into things, we focus on words and slide decks, instead of connection. We get tangled up in knots concerned about ourselves and neglect the part that needs things to be accessible, meaningful and impactful. The point of influence is to mobilise people to *do* stuff. Unfortunately, that requires more than talk – it needs us to be intentional about connection.

The single biggest problem in communication is the illusion that it has taken place.

George Bernard Shaw

I once worked with a government agency on a new organisational strategy, where a spectacular effort went into communicating the new direction across the organisation. Once confirmed, a series of roadshows took place across the country. More than 5000 staff attended over several days to hear about the new strategy, understand what it meant for them, watch videos and connect with their peers. Everything looked great – until the chief executive took the stage.

After a compelling and inspiring address about the purpose and importance of their work, the chief executive then outlined the pillars of the new strategy – resilient and diverse communities, social and economic wellbeing and a strong national identity. Nothing wrong with that. The problem came next when he paused at the end and asked: 'So, what do you think? Did we miss anything?'

It took everything I had not to head-butt the wall next to me. All that energy, only to undermine the message in one fell swoop. As politely as I could manage, I took the chief executive aside after his first presentation to have a few words. I let him know that telling people about a new direction and then undermining it by asking if its right is a bit dumb. If you didn't engage with parts of your business to develop your priorities and direction in the first place, it's a bit late now! Asking for feedback you don't intend to use is bad practice. Also, if the outcome of the roadshows was engagement and ownership, all of the communication needs to point to that purpose.

It's critical to be crystal clear on what you're doing before you communicate. Are you providing information, making meaning or providing support? Once you know, they will too.

Influential communication is much simpler than we make it. When in doubt, aim for just three things:

1. First, be clear. If you can only do one thing, devote your energy to making your ideas accessible, meaningful and easy to understand.
2. Next, be real. Authenticity, credibility and likeability go a long way.
3. Last, be interesting. Grab attention and be relevant, but only once you've got the first two puzzle pieces in place.

If we can do all three, our communication is credible, authentic and memorable.

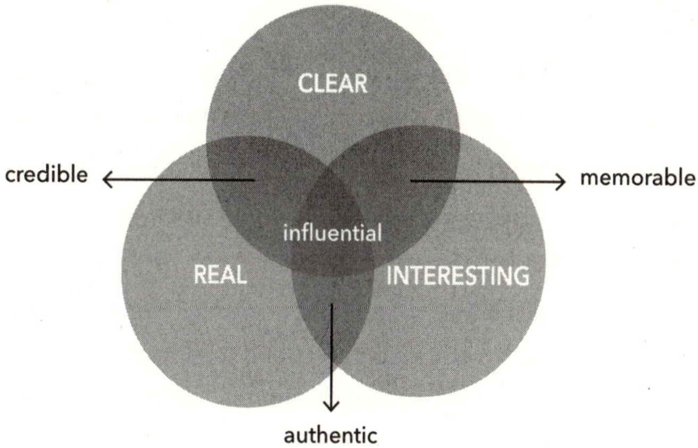

Be clear

During the COVID-19 lockdown, my team experienced a rapid shift in operating model. In just a couple of weeks, we went from running training and workshops in rooms full of people, to delivering online. We've learned a lot on our journey – more than I could list here – but one lesson has stuck with me.

One of the most challenging skills required for running online workshops and webinars is the ability to shut up after you ask a question and stop trying to fill the gap. The temptation, during the 15 seconds of uncomfortable silence, is to ask a question four times in rapid succession because you're scared no-one will engage. This is a mistake.

The most useful communication skill I've learned in this context is to ask a one-line question clearly and then shut up and smile, waiting for people to answer. Anything extra you say is noise, and it's confusing.

People need time to process what you've got to say. Being succinct, staying on message and using as few words as possible is harder than the alternative, but it's worth the effort. As Blaise Pascal once said, 'I would have written a shorter letter, but I did not have the time'.

How can you say less in a way that means more?

Be real

If I met your senior leadership team and asked what your organisation's strategy is, how many different answers would I get?

It's hard to respond to complicated questions with simple answers. It's even harder to answer simple questions when all we have are complicated answers.

Somewhere along the way, we let buzzwords take over. Senior leaders and chief executives are walking around talking about objectives, missions, visions, purpose, strategies, approaches, principles, values, action plans and initiatives – it's enough to give anyone a headache.

Using language that people can connect with is one of the most effective ways to establish trust and build a positive reputation. It's all about 'processing fluency' – familiarity makes it easy to trust what you're saying.

People use complicated language because they think it adds to their credibility, but the opposite is true. The more concrete language you use (think less jargon and fewer buzzwords), the more trustworthy and truthful your statements appear. Governments across the world know this – including New Zealand, which supports the Plain English Awards. Companies have figured it out, too – British Telecom claims to have cut customer queries by 25 per cent by switching to plain English!

Have you ever heard the saying, 'If you can't explain it to a six-year-old, you don't understand it yourself'? This is a lot like that. Jargon is a clear sign we don't know what we're on about.

Where could you use more plain English?

Be interesting

We need to stop interrupting what people are interested in and be what people are interested in.

David Beebe

Every time I walk into a workshop with a new group, I have two important jobs to get out of the way before we can get to work:

1. Establish credibility.
2. Generate interest.

Is this partly because I'm a young chick with far too much energy instead of a boring old dude? Yes.

But more than that, it's because I'm usually there to talk about strategy and change, and both of those get a bad rap. People think they're boring topics (though I disagree!), so I need to quickly connect and build rapport on the things that people care about to get them to pay attention.

In our desire to be professional, many of us have sucked away our personalities, saving them for Friday night drinks. But being authentic doesn't need to mean unprofessional, and being interesting doesn't need to mean showing off. Instead, in a world full of spin and fake news, it's about capturing the interest of your jaded, sceptical audience.

Believe this: you are already interesting. The things you care about, your hobbies and your personality traits make you an interesting person – it's hiding them under a veneer that makes you boring. Being interesting is not about performance; it's connection. Tap into what makes you you, and provide an opportunity for others to do the same.

What opportunities do you have to be more... you?

What we've learned so far

- Leaders need followers if they want their ideas to have impact at scale.
- We can all be influencers, if we're likeable and communicate well.
- Our intent needs to be in the right place, so we can serve the people we're talking to.

Your next step

Identify opportunities in your upcoming meetings or presentations to intentionally communicate with more clarity, authenticity and interest.

LESSON 16

Nurture your network

We're living in the age of networks. All of us have them: personal and professional, digital and tangible, internal and external.

Understanding your network, your role in it and your personal influence style is critical to be a strategic influencer. If you work your network, your ideas are more likely to be supported by others. You'll have better access to resources, support and information, and you'll save time by knowing where to go with tricky questions. You'll be more aware of what's going on around you, and you'll start to get a birds-eye view – helping you spot opportunities and problems more easily.

In my work with teams and leaders, I've noticed several varieties of influencers:

- *The expert* – the trusted authority who connects people through knowledge and insight. Experts become the 'go-to' with strong currency in technical and scientific-based organisations.

- *The boss* – the strong leader who connects people by virtue of their authority and presence.
- *The broker* – the liaison leader whose work requires them to move between different groups. Often an internal or shared service provider, the broker closes triangles and connects people who should know each other.
- *The other woman* – an externally facing leader who works in multi-stakeholder environments and makes the right internal and external connections.
- *The unicorn* – the rare influencer, probably in the magic 3 per cent, who seems to know what's going on with everything all the time and is recognised as such. Unicorns have deep institutional knowledge and they are often the ones to receive curly questions about history or how things are done.

Influential leaders are clear on which role they play from the list above. Their role might change depending on which network of people they're operating in, and they maximise the opportunities that come from that.

Reflect on your role in your team or organisation - are you the expert, the broker, the boss, the other woman or the unicorn?

DRAW THE MAP

Not everyone is going to love us, and that's cool. There are one billion Apple users, but only a handful of them sleep outside the store when a new iPhone is released. There are Apple haters, too, but they number even fewer and are mostly listened to by other haters. Most people are quietly supporting the brand by handing over their money, using their phones and keeping their mouths shut. Relationships are the same.

When you try to be everything to everyone you risk becoming nothing to no-one. Intentional influencers are clear and honest about who they connect with, and what for. They don't want to waste time trying to make everyone happy; they focus on making sure they've got good relationships in places that really matter. Remember our micro-influencers? It's all about quality, not quantity.

Every leader should know what their network looks like: who they're connected to (personally *and* professionally), what the value of that relationship is and how important it is to the big picture. This isn't grubby, or transactional – it's a sensible, clean way to be intentional and genuine in your connections.

Try drawing up your network map, with a series of post-it notes. On each note mark what the value of that relationship is, why you need to keep it (or not) and how you should keep the relationship going. Think about your most important goals for the future and identify any gaps, or relationships that might require more investment. This clarity should help you make decisions about where to direct your energy, so that you don't drop important balls.

For bonus points, consider the dynamics of each of those relationships, and what each person or stakeholder most needs from you. Influence isn't just about you – it's a reciprocal dance that should help everyone achieve their goals by leveraging others' efforts.

For example, the team you manage needs your direction and support the most. With that clarity, you can tailor your communication to be as clear and directive as possible, asking good questions about their challenges. Your colleagues, however, don't need you to tell them what to do. Instead, they value your perspective, reciprocity and flexibility. For these relationships you should go out of your way to listen, and be flexible whenever you can.

The dynamic with your superiors is different again. Building credible influence with managers needs you to establish two-way trust and offer solutions, not problems. In that dynamic, problem-solving positions you as a trusted go-to. Try that same behaviour with your teams, though, and you're edging into micromanaging territory. Senior leaders need your expertise and insight, so your interactions should reflect that – but flex your expertise with your peers, and you could get them offside.

The key is to be as intentional as possible, honouring the time and investment of everyone you're connected to.

Take the time to map your network, considering intention, connection and relationship dynamics. Why are you connecting? What does that relationship need? Where are your gaps?

DIG A LITTLE DEEPER

Some people just feel like problems, don't they? They're annoying. They don't buy in. They put up barriers when you're trying to keep things moving forward. They ask too many questions, send too many emails and don't get moving fast enough.

Well, when you take people at face value, sure. But when you assume positive intent and focus on *interpreting* people's behaviour, rather than absorbing it, you can build a more connected and nuanced relationship. When you're confronted with someone who seems resistant or difficult, try asking bigger questions. What do they need? What are they afraid of? What is holding them back?

In my workshops, we often run an exercise called 'Fresh Perspective' where attendees choose a different person to be and try to see the world through their eyes.

If the finance team members are slow to adopt our new software and are making life harder than it needs to be, it's easy to get frustrated. Why are they so resistant to change? Why don't they realise how important this is? In other words: Why doesn't everyone care as much as I do about the thing I know or care the most about?

Using Fresh Perspective, we seek to understand by asking what the team might be saying, doing, feeling and thinking. As an exercise in empathy mapping, this line of questioning puts us in another's shoes.

Influence: a case study

Let's imagine for a moment we're playing Fresh Perspective, and Barry from the finance team is the person we've chosen to empathy map. We would ask what Barry might be *doing, saying, thinking and feeling* to understand how to keep things moving forward.

What is Barry doing?

Not turning up to meetings; continuing to use the old platform even though it takes longer and is less accurate; replying late to emails.

Why?

He's two staff members down at the moment, it's budget time, and the team is under pressure.

What is Barry saying?

'I don't have time for this.'

'It won't stick.'

What is Barry thinking?

'Another new thing that will be a half-implemented disaster and take me weeks to learn, when I'm already two staff members down and struggling.'

'If I ride this out, it will go away.'

What is Barry feeling?

Frustrated; overwhelmed; unheard; unsupported.

In Barry's case, asking better questions helps to develop our perspective and diffuse some of the initial frustration we're feeling. It allows us to take agency of our side of the equation and shift the only thing we actually have control over: our own behaviour. If the point of new software is to make Barry's life easier, have we made that clear? Have we acknowledged his concerns, clearly outlined the benefits and provided the support necessary to make it work in his team? If he's already two staff members down, learning a new tool will be tricky, but worth it if it's a timesaver. Can we create better training resources to make it easy? Could we provide an IT person to sit with the finance team for half a day at the next budget round, and set up a good feedback loop to make sure the new system is working for them?

And the most important question: does he have a point?

Usually, difficult people are onto something that we've missed.

Are you dealing with a resistant or challenging person in your work or personal life? How can you take their perspective to understand them better? What could you change in that dynamic?

BELIEVE THE DIFFICULT

If you hate conflict, you're not alone. Most people will do everything they can to avoid awkward and tense conversations. If you're a leader, you're out of luck. Assume there's conflict in your future, and that you'd better be ready to handle it.

Very few people get up in the morning wanting to be unhelpful, cynical or disengaged. Most people are motivated to do good in the world and to find a way to do that.

Difficult people are usually difficult for a reason. The magic comes when we're able to suspend our own ego and engage with conflicting views. When we do that, we improve the quality of our decisions, expose deficiencies in our plans and make our thinking more relevant. More than that, when we engage the difficult people they often become our biggest allies.

Just like the approach we took with Barry in finance, dealing with problem people is not about silencing dissent – it's about understanding it. Whether we like it or not, negative and disengaged people can have a significant impact on projects and workplaces, even when others don't pay them much heed. Criticism or apathy creates a toxic environment that can make progress hard. Most of the time, these people see something we don't – and if they're saying it, you'd better believe that others are thinking it.

What are your cynics seeing that you're not? Is your ego getting in the way?

A word of warning, though: before going to the effort to placate a difficult stakeholder, carefully consider how much time and energy to exert. Not all cynics are created equally, and it's easy to wind up in a loop where we're serving the squeakiest wheel, but not moving forward.

Consider the relative power and interest of your stakeholders to understand how to tackle cynics. If they're exerting real influence on the people you need on your side, then invest the time. If they're grumbly but have little or no impact, do the bare minimum, or try to remove them from the project or workplace entirely.

How powerful are your cynics? Who most needs your time and attention?

EARN YOUR ENGAGEMENT

Imagine proposing marriage on the first introduction.

At an after-dinner conference speech last year, I had attendees do just that – to the person sitting next to them. Unsurprisingly it was a bit of a leap, even for those who already knew each other. The exercise was a useful prod, to demonstrate the awkward reality of expecting loyalty from the first moment. We go into change and engagement processes at work all the time expecting this kind of immediate commitment.

Assume that no-one cares what you have to say. They're busy, they're overwhelmed and they're fighting their own battles. The bar is high, and you need to respect their time as well as yours. Matt Church, one of Australia's top motivational speakers, warns public speakers to remember three key things:

1. They're not listening.
2. They don't care.
3. You don't matter.

It's true: getting people's attention is hard work. Researchers at the University of Denmark have found that our *collective* attention span is shorter than ever. The rapidly accelerating amount of content being produced and consumed means we've got less space, and that our attention is exhausted much faster.

To get that attention requires more than obligation – it needs inspiration.

SELL BENEFITS, NOT FEATURES

One of the most useful professional development courses I've done was as a 17-year-old, working in an electronics store. In an introductory three-day sales course, the trainer hammered home early on: everything is sales, and everyone is a salesperson – but some of us are better at it than others. Having good products and knowing the right information will never be enough to meet our targets, so our sales success rests on our ability to truly understand our customers and what they really need.

Sales gets a bad rap, and many people consider themselves above it. Imagine their surprise when they learn that 40 per cent of the average workday is spent selling. For some, that's sales in a traditional sense – products, services, programmes – but for many it's more about selling ourselves or our ideas.

Once we know something, we make assumptions about how well it is already understood – which also means we underestimate the work needed to convince others it's a good idea. Chip and Dan Heath call this 'the Curse of Knowledge'. We need to make sure we can clearly communicate why our thing is so important, so we can connect others to its benefits, too.

When I was selling cameras, that meant talking about benefits instead of features: people buy cameras to capture precious moments with their loved ones, not to have the fastest shutter speed. When you're influencing to drive change, the most important question is: 'What's in it for them?'

Ask yourself: Why is it worth people's while listening to you? Will working with you give them more time, more money or more status? Is it about saving time, reducing frustration or making their job easier? Focus on the positive outcomes you're working to deliver together.

How can you sell others on the benefits of your idea? What's in it for them?

CREATE OWNERSHIP

In my sales days, we also learned a lot about the importance of asking for the sale. It's all very well selling a customer on the camera's benefits, but most people still won't purchase until the salesperson makes an explicit invitation. We make the same problem in the workplace: we get people excited, but we don't make it easy for them to get involved.

For change at scale, people need an invitation to action and the opportunity for ownership.

We can't own what we didn't make. In *Drive: The Surprising Truth About What Motivates Us*, Daniel Pink argues that an extrinsic 'carrot and stick' approach only drives performance and change for basic, mechanical tasks. For anything that requires decision-making and creativity, motivation needs to be intrinsic and is all about autonomy, mastery and purpose.

Activating others requires all three – a clear and important outcome, the ability to own it and create excellence.

Have you given people a chance to shape their own future? How could you?

BUILD A TRIBE

The secret of leadership is simple: Do what you believe in. Paint a picture. Go there. People will follow.

Seth Godin

People have an innate need to belong. According to Matthew Lieberman, connecting with others is a primary need – more fundamental than food or shelter. Creating tribes is an essential part of life, and when we build groups of people defined by their connection, we feel better. It's why we join teams, clubs and Facebook pages. It's the reason we gather at Christmas, go to work lunches and commit to communities of practice. It feels good to belong.

Seth Godin is the godfather of modern tribe-building. In *Tribes: We Need You to Lead Us*, he argues that, 'A group needs only two things to be a tribe: a shared interest and a way to communicate'. As a leader, uniting people around a common purpose creates the opportunity to turn a shared idea into a movement. Building an engaged, aligned tribe is a powerful way to unleash your impact at scale.

In our 'Fast Forward' programme, we harness the power of a tribe to keep change moving. From visible indicators like lanyards and ID cards through to participation in online and in-person communities, the markers of belonging to a group provide a sense of positive peer pressure, keeping people accountable and on track throughout an accelerated change programme over eight weeks. After graduating, each participant becomes a Fast Forward alumni member, with the opportunity to mentor future cohorts through the process. At the end of each cohort, the feedback is always clear: people appreciated the opportunity to connect with others and be part of something. When they came up against obstacles, the support and accountability of their tribe kept them moving. Managers have staff, but leaders have followers. Leaders have followers, but influential leaders have tribes.

How are you building yours?

GO BEYOND TEAMWORK

Ah, collaboration – one of the most overused buzzwords of the early 2000s. While any initiative or team with more than three people lays claim to it, real collaboration is different from run-of-the-mill teamwork. Teamwork is about people in similar areas, or with similar skills, achieving a shared goal. Collaboration is about harnessing diversity: bringing people with *different* skillsets and expertise together to create new value, with a shared goal in mind. It's about achieving more than the sum of your parts.

When collaboration works, it's great. We can be more productive, make progress more quickly and develop more comprehensive and nuanced solutions. Those results aren't guaranteed, though. Good collaboration needs a particular skillset that goes beyond regular team leadership. You need to have clear expectations, defined roles and responsibilities, an organised process and the right tools and resources.

Most of all, collaboration fails when people feel like they aren't being listened to, their opinion isn't valued or their contribution isn't acknowledged. Committed leadership, regular check-ins and honest troubleshooting is the ticket – which means making sure you schedule team meetings for progress checks, not just decision-making.

Are you confusing teamwork with collaboration? Find ways to add more diversity to the mix and structure your process for success.

PUT SOME SKIN IN THE GAME

Relationships and partnerships are different beasts. When we confuse the two, or promise something we can't deliver on, trust erodes quickly, making it hard to get anywhere. At its heart, the difference between a relationship and a partnership is skin in the game. Everyone in the room needs to have a stake in the outcome and the ability to shape the pathway. When leaders or organisations are afraid to surrender power and control, they hamstring the ability of a group to affect real change. The public sector is particularly bad at this. Councils ask for community ownership but provide no delegation or authority. Governments ask for commercial cooperation but remove all profit margins from contracts that expire too regularly to incentivise sustainably. True partnerships require trust and meaningful autonomy to work.

Make no mistake: partnerships are hard work. Sharing power makes decisions more challenging and complex. We have to give up some control. There are competing interests to balance, and information needs to be shared. While this takes longer, if done well it lives on much longer, too.

Are you confusing relationships with partnerships? How can you make sure everyone has some skin in the game?

What we've learned so far

- Developing intentional networks is an honest way to build meaningful relationships.
- Difficult people are usually like that for a reason.
- We're all salespeople.
- Ownership requires invitation.
- Collaboration is more than teamwork.

Your next step

Map your network – who you're connected to and why, and what they need from you. Identify your gaps.

CHEAT SHEET

INFLUENCE

What we've learned

I've worked in and around politics for most of my career. I'm always fascinated by people's attitudes towards it. Most people tend to think they're 'above' politics, or that it's dirty, so they don't play the game.

This is a mistake. Performance alone isn't enough to get you noticed or bring people along with you. Influence is about understanding relationships, networks and people, and using that knowledge to have real impact.

Embracing and understanding politics is a non-negotiable skillset for strategic leaders who want to have an impact at scale. Resisting politics shuts down opportunities and keeps us out of conversations where we could make a big difference.

The problem with politics is when it gets slimy – but it doesn't have to. Political and social intelligence require learning, practice and intentional behaviour. How slimy you are is entirely up to you.

Being savvy is not synonymous with being slimy – there are clear differences. While slimy influencers are manipulative and disingenuous, savvy influencers lead from an authentic viewpoint, to inspire others. Where slimy leaders are calculated, savvy leaders are considered.

Slimy leaders change what they're saying based on who they're talking to, but savvy leaders stay flexible and open to others' thinking. They understand that their approach will need to change depending on who they're with and what they need – but it doesn't make them fake. Savvy influencers don't compromise on the important stuff, and they're authentic when it counts.

Ultimately, it comes down to the same two things: intent and impact. If your intention is in the right place, and you're aiming for the right thing, you're not being slimy. Go with your gut; you'll know when you cross the line. Above all:

- Show *respect* by understanding what you need from others and what they need from you.
- Show *empathy* by identifying the needs, fears and desires of your disengaged stakeholders.
- Show *authenticity* by communicating in ways that reach people.
- Show *passion* by making your ideas meaningful and interesting.
- Show *trust* to build ownership and drive change.
- Show *integrity* to build sustainable momentum.

Here are a few attributes of slimy versus savvy leaders:

Slimy leaders	**Savvy leaders**
Are charismatic	Are authentic
Change others	Change themselves
Manipulate	Inspire
Trade in favours	Trade in ideas
Attract followers	Build tribes

What you can do

Take the time to consider how important it is for your ideas to take on a life of their own. How much of a difference would it make to your work if you had a tribe of believers and strong relationships that supported your efforts?

Consider the level of influence you need to have in the future and start to build those relationships now. Map your network, prioritise time for connecting regularly with your most valued contacts and make a concerted effort to forge new connections in important areas.

Remember that difficult people are usually that way for a reason. The next time you find yourself frustrated, take a step back. Ask yourself:

- Why are they doing this?
- What are they afraid of?
- What do they need?
- What are they seeing that I'm not?

By cultivating an openness to diverse perspectives, you will deepen your own trust and credibility, as well as strengthening the quality of your ideas.

It's time to start building your tribe, so that your thinking can get out of your head and take on a life of its own. It's not easy - getting people's attention is tricky, and it requires you to let go, but once you do that, you'll feel the shift in your environment.

Look for opportunities to build connection and belonging into your current projects and teams. How can you make sure people are inspired, and understand the importance of the work you are trying to engage them with?

Most importantly, remember: you don't need to be a charismatic extrovert to be an influencer, but you do need to be likeable. The 'professional' facades we put up at work usually act as barriers to connection, so put your guard down once in a while. Be you, be nice and care about others - it goes a long way.

Three key questions

1. Am I likeable?
2. What do they need?
3. Why should they care?

WHERE TO FROM HERE?

How good would it be if knowing better meant doing better?

Unfortunately, that's not how things work – at least not things that matter. The ongoing gap between what we know and what we do is the intractable battle of being human.

We don't know the future. Nobody does. Change is never going to be *done*, whether it's in us or around us. We're all perpetually unfinished projects. As soon as we're better, we see how much further there is to go. Sometimes that hits out of nowhere. It's big, obvious, jarring, inescapable and turns everything upside down. Change or bust.

Other times, though, it isn't like that at all. Sometimes the signs that we've reached the ceiling of our efforts are small. They're quiet, insidious and shifty, and these are the times we need to be most careful about. It's much easier to be a hero in a crisis than it is to be open, aware and committed in the calm. It's easy to push for transformation when the shit hits the fan. When we capsize, we can dig deep to find the best version of ourselves. It's much harder to rock the boat when everything is going OK.

Government has twigged, and they're trying something new. In New Zealand, this is best demonstrated by the passage of the new Public Service Act in late 2020. The Act is a significant shift towards more adaptive and collaborative leadership of the public service, joining up agencies in outcomes-focused boards and entities and requiring a more strategic approach to leadership development. This is a fantastic sign, after decades of contractual, siloed public management, which can be seen in every corner of the world. It's not just government that needs to learn these lessons, though. Any single actor can't solve our most wicked problems in isolation. They need the input and foresight of leaders across the board – government, business, communities and individuals. The COVID-19 pandemic has made this more obvious than ever.

It's not going to be easy. We need a completely different approach to tackling the hardest, deepest, ugliest stuff – the stuff that doesn't feel good to acknowledge and is easier to put in the too-hard basket. It's an uncomfortable dissonance, isn't it?

A new commitment is needed to tackle what lies beneath the surface. We need a real acknowledgement of how we keep setting ourselves up to fail – whether it's because we don't understand the challenges in front of us, we don't know how to work together or we don't know how to do things any differently. It's time. The stakes are high and the conditions are right. Before the memory of our latest crisis fades, we need to commit.

It's OK to change things. It's OK to change ourselves. We've all been battling away, with flaws and unintended consequences, and that's OK too. The way we are now is rarely the result of ineptitude or personal failing. The way we are now is rarely unreasonable. Our 'now' is the way we've had to respond in the past, for reasons that make sense, and it served us – until it didn't.

And it doesn't anymore. The future, which we never know and never will, depends on showing courage – making a commitment to work together, put away the scorecard and self-protection, and close the gap between what we think and what we do. We need to stop pointing the finger and hiding behind our titles, our identities, our barriers and our differences and get real about change.

The next is here. The new is within reach.

But there's work to do.

We can't just rely on ourselves to be different. We can't be trusted. The key lies in asking trickier questions, committing to growth and designing our environments in a way that makes it easier to do the right thing.

With that in mind, the answer lies in how we train and support our leaders. What behaviours will we reward, and how? What are the expectations of our time and output, and is there a built-in tolerance for, and encouragement of, experimentation and flexibility?

On an individual level, embedding these behaviours means:

- *Taking control of your time and attention.* What gets scheduled gets done. Eliminate distractions, overwhelm and noise by communicating your needs and expectations clearly and empowering others to do the same.
- *Changing how you make decisions* by carving out half a day every week for thinking; setting up early warning signals; and requiring genuine options, meaningful recommendations and critical thought from your teams.
- *Creating prompts and systems* that tackle problems and performance issues with better questions. One of my mentees puts post-it notes with challenging questions on her computer monitor as a reminder to ask them in meetings. Over time, this becomes a habit.
- *Prioritising relationships, conversations, and connection,* rather than expecting it to happen by accident. Building stakeholder planning into all significant projects. Budgeting for implementation, rollout and behaviour change.

- *Investing in growth and development* by reading, attending webinars and conferences, and inviting new thinkers and speakers into your organisation to trigger insights and open doors.

On a broader scale, making a new vision of leadership a reality means:

- *Changing the way we train and develop people* to prioritise the skills and behaviours that we need the most: flexibility, decision-making, systems thinking, performance and influence.
- *Embedding those priorities* into a clear, coherent development pathway, with assessments and applications that support your organisational goals for the future.
- *Changing reward, recognition and performance frameworks* to make long-term gains more attractive than short-term wins, and incentivise meaningful collaboration and genuine systems change.
- *Creating the space and expectation,* through meeting cadences and scheduling guidelines, to provide time for the work that really matters.
- *Adjusting decision, strategy and funding processes* to build in space for iteration, piloting and experimentation.

JUST START. NOW.

Learning a language is significantly easier if you hear it spoken early in life.

Babies are born with special skills for language acquisition, which are hard at work before they can even speak. Before they turn one, babies can differentiate between all sounds across all languages. Then, depending on the languages they are exposed to, this ability is pared back until they can discern only those sounds necessary for them to create meaning. Dr Paul Thompson, a neurology professor at UCLA, found that the brain systems that specialise in learning new languages grow rapidly from around six years of age until the onset of puberty. But then these systems seem to shut down and stop growing from age 11 to 15. That's not to say it's too late to re-acquire this ability.

As an adult, learning a new skill, response or language is hard. You need to compare new experiences, meanings and sounds to your native language. Once you're an adult, many of the neural pathways that would have helped have already been sealed off. Un-learning and re-learning are significantly more challenging than fresh learning, whether it's language or leadership. For many of you, leading differently isn't just about learning – it's about un-learning, too.

At some level, we do this already. Most people, as they move through the ranks, need to change what they focus on. What makes a good team leader or supervisor is not the same as what makes a good executive. The problem is when we try to bring the old skills forward and *add* a few, rather than engaging in the process of un-learning and re-learning the skills that will make us most effective in our new role or environment. Letting go of what made us great is hard.

Because of this we find leaders at the executive level trying desperately to cling to their subject matter expertise and use that to solve problems. That prevents the people they lead from applying their skills to new challenges, limits their autonomy and makes it difficult for teams to grow. It's a tricky spot to be in. When we've been promoted for how well we did at our last level of seniority, it's tough to give up what we've been rewarded for. And the longer we spend at one level, the harder it is to adjust to the next.

It takes flexibility to stay relevant and make a difference. You need to grow, innovate and change – almost daily. Realising that and developing the necessary skillset will save you significant time and pain. In a world that is full of leaders clinging to what got them to the top, you'll also have a distinct advantage.

PRACTICE MAKES... AUTOPILOT

If you've attended a training course or conference lately you'll know how tiring learning can be. Taking on new information and getting our heads around new skills is exhausting. It requires us to switch off autopilot and keep all systems firing.

Anything worth learning has a steep effort curve at the beginning. Whether it's driving, playing an instrument or taking on new practices at work, the initial steps are foreign and challenging – and there's no autopilot to guide you. For leaders who need to continually think differently about new problems and be focused and strategic in their work, every day can feel like a battle.

The good news is that the learning curve, like the challenges we're tackling, is often nonlinear. In *Atomic Habits*, James Clear talks about the lag effect of small changes that create big transformation. By taking the right steps and consistently focusing on specific behaviours, big change becomes possible. This is true of our personal habits, and of rolling out organisational change.

We are what we repeatedly do.
Excellence, then, is not an act, but a habit.

Will Durant

According to Clear, we often give up just before we reach the tipping point – where all those incremental, consistent changes make everything easier. Once these new habits are embedded, like driving or playing an instrument, we get to shift those behaviours into the autopilot zone and focus on something else.

Nothing worth having ever comes easy. If we want something new and better, we need to learn how to *be* new and better. Practise is the key. It might not make perfect, but it can make autopilot. And that's enough.

ABOUT THE AUTHOR

New Zealand's leading voice on strategy, change and leadership, Alicia McKay doesn't waste time with buzzwords and bullshit.

New Zealand and Australia's most senior leaders call on Alicia when they need to think big, make hard decisions and transform their teams, organisations and communities. Working with Alicia is a game-changer. She's known for sparking seismic shifts in people, strategy, communication and culture. Alicia is an expert in strategic decision-making and problem-solving, drawing on rich experience working with executive teams as well as holding accreditations in better business cases, managing benefits and investment logic mapping.

Passionate about supporting motivated people to do work that matters – in even the most challenging environments – Alicia's unique approach transforms frustrated leaders and teams. Certified Leadership Versatility Index (LVI 360) assessor and self-confessed leadership nerd, Alicia's proven method to build sustainable skills of the future is changing the way people think, lead and learn.

Co-host of the *What's on Your Mind?* podcast and author of *From Strategy to Action: A Guide to Getting Shit Done in the Public Sector*, Alicia keeps it real, bringing fresh thinking and sharp insight to audiences across the globe from her home in Wellington, New Zealand.

When she's not working, reading, thinking or speaking, she enjoys spending time with her three daughters, running next to the water, yelling at the radio and spending time with friends.

Alicia is also a sought-after speaker for conferences and events. Funny, fresh and impossibly real, Alicia cuts through the crap and makes sense of things in a way audiences love.

Learn more about Alicia at www.aliciamckay.co.nz.

WHAT I'M READING

Done, but still hungry? I get it: as soon as you know a little something, you realise how much more there still is to learn.

I read a lot of books. I devoured an obscene number in the research phase of this book. I'm no librarian, but if you want to learn more about some of the things I've talked about, I can personally recommend the following texts for further learning.

On complexity and the world in general

Harari, Yuval Noah (2018). *Homo Deus: A brief history of tomorrow.* Harper Perennial.

Raworth, Kate (2018). *Doughnut Economics: Seven Ways to Think Like a 21st Century Economist.* Random House Business.

Rösling, Hans, Rösling, O & Rönnlund, AR (2018). *Factfulness: Ten reasons we're wrong about the world – and why things are better than you think.* Flatiron Books.

Taleb, N Nicholas (2016). *Antifragile: Things that Gain from Disorder.* Random House.

On adaptive leadership

Goldsmith, Marshall (2014). *What Got You Here Won't Get You There: How successful people become even more successful.* Hachette Books.

Heifetz, Ronald A, Grashow, A & Linsky, M (2009). *The Practice of Adaptive Leadership: Tools and tactics for changing your organization and the world.* Harvard Business Press.

Montgomery, Cynthia (2013). *The Strategist: Be the leader your business needs.* Collins.

Pressfield, Steven (2012). *Turning Pro.* Black Irish Entertainment.

Sinek, Simon (2011). *Start With Why: How great leaders inspire everyone to take action.* Penguin.

On flexibility

Holiday, Ryan (2015). *The Obstacle is the Way: The ancient art of turning adversity to advantage.* Profile Books.

Kaplan, Robert E & Kaiser, Robert B (2013). *Fear Your Strengths: What you are best at could be your biggest problem.* Berrett-Koehler Publishers.

On decisions

Ariely, Dan (2010). *Predictably Irrational: The hidden forces that shape our decisions.* Harper Perennial.

Ertel, Chris & Solomon, Lisa Kay (2014). *Moments of Impact: How to design strategic conversations that accelerate change.* Simon & Schuster.

Kahneman, Daniel (2011). *Thinking, fast and slow.* Farrar, Straus and Giroux.

McGrath, Rita (2019). *Seeing Around Corners: how to spot inflection points in business before they happen.* Houghton Mifflin Harcourt.

McKeown, Max (2020). *The Strategy Book: How to think and act strategically to deliver outstanding results.* Pearson.

Riel, Jennifer & Martin, RL (2017). *Creating Great Choices: A leader's guide to integrative thinking.* Harvard Business Review Press.

Syed, Matthew (2020). *Rebel Ideas: The power of diverse thinking.* John Murray Publishers Ltd.

On systems

King, Stephen (2011). *11/22/63: A novel.* Scribner.

McKey, Zoe (2018). *Think in systems: complexity made simple: the theory and practice of strategic planning, problem solving, and creating lasting results.* Createspace Independent Publishing Platform.

Thaler, Richard H & Sunstein, Cass R (2009). *Nudge: improving decisions about health, wealth, and happiness.* Penguin Books.

On performance

Anthony, Scott D, Gilbert, CG & Johnson, MW (2017). *Dual transformation: how to reposition today's business while creating the future.* Harvard Business Review Press.

Clear, James (2018). *Atomic Habits: An easy & proven way to build good habits and break bad ones.* Avery.

Cloud, Henry (2010). *Necessary Endings: the employees, businesses, and relationships that all of us have to give up in order to move forward.* HarperCollins.

McKeown, Greg (2014*). Essentialism: the disciplined pursuit of less.* Virgin Books.

Pink, Daniel H (2017). *When: The scientific secrets of perfect timing.* Riverhead Books.

On influence

Cialdini, Robert (1993). *Influence: Science and practice.* HarperCollins College.

Godin, Seth (2008). *Tribes: We Need You to Lead Us.* Portfolio.

Hatton, Shane (2019). *Lead the Room.* Major Street Publishing.

Heath, Chip & Heath, Dan (2007). *Made to Stick: Why some ideas survive and others die.* Random House.

Heath, Chip & Heath, Dan (2017). *The Power of Moments: Why certain experiences have extraordinary impact.* Simon & Schuster.

Pink, Daniel H (2012). *To Sell is Human: The surprising truth about moving others.* Riverhead Books.

Other books I think everyone should read

Eddo-Lodhe, Reni (2018). *Why I'm No Longer Talking to White People About Race.* Bloomsbury Publishing.

Giridharadas, Anand (2019). *Winners Take All: The Elite Charade of Changing the World.* Random House.

Gladwell, Malcolm (2019). *Talking to Strangers: What we should know about the people we don't know.* Allen Lane.

Haidt, Jonathan (2012). *The righteous mind: Why good people are divided by politics and religion.* Pantheon Books.

Jay, Meg (2018). *Supernormal: Childhood adversity and the untold story of resilience.* Canongate Books.

McGarvey, Darren (2018). *Poverty Safari: understanding the anger of Britain's underclass.* Picador.

REFERENCES

Preface

Gladwell, Malcolm (2011). *Outliers: The Story of Success.* Back Bay Books.

Kasriel, Stephane (2017). 'Skill, re-skill and re-skill again. How to keep up with the future of work'. World Economic Forum. weforum.org/agenda/2017/07/skill-reskill-prepare-for-future-of-work.

Introduction

Manson, Mark (2020). Twitter. twitter.com/iammarkmanson/status/1262467681749524480.

Miller, Donald (2011). *A Million Miles in a Thousand Years: How I Learned to Live a Better Story.* Thomas Nelson.

Koehn, Nancy F (2017). *Forged in Crisis: The Power of Courageous Leadership in Turbulent Times.* Scribner.

Young, Jeffrey R (2017). 'How Many Times Will People Change Jobs? The Myth of the Endlessly-Job-Hopping Millennial'. EdSurge. edsurge.com/news/2017-07-20-how-many-times-will-people-change-jobs-the-myth-of-the-endlessly-job-hopping-millennial.

Scott, Digby (2016). 'Work with the patterns'. digbyscott.com/2016/03/08/see-the-patterns-use-the-patterns.

World Economic Forum (2018). 'The Future of Jobs Report'. weforum.org/docs/WEF_Future_of_Jobs_2018.pdf.

Deloitte Insights (2020). *The Fourth Industrial Revolution: At the Intersection of Readiness and Responsibility.* deloitte.com/content/dam/Deloitte/de/Documents/human-capital/Deloitte_Review_26_Fourth_Industrial_Revolution.pdf.

Kabacoff, Robert (2014). 'Develop Strategic Thinkers Throughout Your Organization'. *Harvard Business Review.* hbr.org/2014/02/develop-strategic-thinkers-throughout-your-organization.

Clark, Dorie (2018). 'If Strategy Is So Important, Why Don't We Make Time For It?' *Harvard Business Review.* hbr.org/2018/06/if-strategy-is-so-important-why-dont-we-make-time-for-it.

Colarelli Beatty, Katherine (2010). 'The Three Strengths Of A True Strategic Leader'. *Forbes.* forbes.com/2010/10/27/three-strengths-strategy-leadership-managing-ccl.html?sh=1ebcba365280.

Prereading

Clear, James (2018). *Atomic Habits: An easy and proven way to build good habits and break bad ones.* Avery.

Tugend, Alina (2011). *Better by Mistake: The Unexpected Benefits of Being Wrong.* Riverhead Books.

Covey, Steven R (2004). *The 7 habits of highly effective people: Restoring the character ethic.* Free Press.

Lesson 1

Kaiser, Robert & Overfield, Darren (2010). 'Assessing flexible leadership as a mastery of opposites'. *Consulting Psychology Journal: Practice and Research*, vol. 62, pp. 105–118.

ANZSOG (2019). 'Today's Problems, Yesterday's Toolkit: Restoring Trust in Government by Reinventing How the Public Service Works'. anzsog.edu.au/resource-library/news-media/todays-problems-yesterdays-toolkit-public-service.

Lesson 2

Norton, Larry (2010). 'Flexible leadership: An integrative perspective'. *Consulting Psychology Journal: Practice and Research*, vol. 62, pp. 143–150.

Eurich, Tasha (2018). 'What Self-Awareness Really Is (and How to Cultivate It)'. *Harvard Business Review*. hbr.org/2018/01/what-self-awareness-really-is-and-how-to-cultivate-it.

Kaiser Leadership. 'Leadership Versatility Index'. lvi.kaiserleadership.com.

Atkin, Christopher & Badham, Stephen (2018). The phenomenological Influence of Inner Speech on Executive Functions. *Journal of Undergraduate Research at NTU*, vol. 1, no. 1, pp. 223–251.

Goleman, Daniel & Boyatzis, Richard E (2008). 'Social Intelligence and the Biology of Leadership'. *Harvard Business Review*. hbr.org/2008/09/social-intelligence-and-the-biology-of-leadership.

Kahneman, Daniel (2011). *Thinking, fast and slow*. Farrar, Straus and Giroux.

Ader, Jill (2020). '3 steps towards enlightened leadership – and career success'. World Economic Forum. weforum.org/agenda/2020/01/leadership-career-success-finding-purpose.

Gino, Francesca (2018). 'The Business Case for Curiosity'. *Harvard Business Review*. hbr.org/2018/09/the-business-case-for-curiosity.

Penman, Danny (2015). *Mindfulness for Creativity: Adapt, create and thrive in a frantic world*. Piatkus.

Belsky, Scott (2020). 'Creativity will be key to competing against AI in the future workforce - here's how'. World Economic Forum. weforum.org/agenda/2020/11/ai-automation-creativity-workforce-skill-fute-of-work.

Lesson 3

Manson, Mark. 'Personal Values: How to Know Who You Really Are'. markmanson.net/personal-values.

Asch, SE (1956). 'Studies of independence and conformity: I. A minority of one against a unanimous majority'. *Psychological Monographs: General and Applied*, vol. 70, no. 9, pp. 1–70.

Edmondson, Amy C (2012). *Teaming: How Organizations Learn, Innovate, and Compete in the Knowledge Economy.* Jossey-Bass.

Lesson 4

Parke, Michael et al. (2018). 'When Daily Planning Improves Employee Performance: The Importance of Planning Type, Engagement, and Interruptions'. *Journal of Applied Psychology*. vol. 103, no. 3, pp. 300–312.

Taleb, Nassim Nicholas (2012). *Antifragile: Things that gain from disorder.* Random House.

Jay, Meg (2017). *Supernormal: The Untold Story of Adversity and Resilience.* Twelve.

Collier, Lorna (2016). 'Growth after trauma: Why are some people more resilient than others—and can it be taught?' American Psychological Association. apa.org/monitor/2016/11/growth-trauma.

Lesson 5

Horwarth, Rich (2008). *Deep Dive: Mastering the Three Disciplines of Strategic Thinking for Competitive Advantage.* Strategic Thinking Institute.

Lesson 6

Taleb, Nassim Nicholas (2007). *The Black Swan: The Impact of the Highly Improbable.* Penguin Press.

William Deresiewicz (2010). 'Solitude and leadership'. The American Scholar. theamericanscholar.org/solitude-and-leadership.

Porter, M and Nitin, N (2018). 'How CEOs Manage Time'. *Harvard Business Review.* hbr.org/2018/07/the-leaders-calendar.

Newman, Leigh (2012). 'Eckhart Tolle: When You Don't Know What to Do'. Ophrah.com. oprah.com/spirit/how-to-make-up-your-mind-decision-making-eckhart-tolle.

Lesson 7

Kahneman, Daniel (2011). *Thinking, fast and slow.* Farrar, Straus and Giroux.

Böckler, Anne et al. (2017). 'Know Thy Selves: Learning to Understand Oneself Increases the Ability to Understand Others'. *Journal of Cognitive Enhancement*, vol. 1, pp. 197–209.

Parkinson, Cyril Northcote (1955). 'Parkinson's Law'. *The Economist.*

GOV.UK (2013). 'Green Book supplementary guidance: optimism bias'. gov.uk/government/publications/green-book-supplementary-guidance-optimism-bias.

Kahneman, Daniel (2011). *Thinking, fast and slow.* Farrar, Straus and Giroux.

Lesson 8

McKeown, Greg (2014). *Essentialism: the disciplined pursuit of less.* Virgin Books.

Lesson 9

Michael Ballé (1996). *Managing With Systems Thinking: Making Dynamics Work for You in Business Decision Making.* Mcgraw Hill Book Co Ltd.

Kauffman, Draper L (1980) *Systems One: An Introduction to Systems Thinking.* Future Systems, Inc.

Hans Rosling (2018). *Factfulness: Ten Reasons We're Wrong About the World – and Why Things Are Better Than You Think.* Sceptre.

Heifetz, RA, Grashow, A & Linsky, M (2009). *The Practice of Adaptive Leadership: Tools and tactics for changing your organisation and the world.* Harvard Business Press.

Stanford University. 'How to identify and remove 5 common causes of organizational drag'. HR Dive. hrdive.com/spons/how-to-identify-and-remove-5-common-causes-of-organizational-drag/428828.

Mankins, Michael (2017). 'Great Companies Obsess Over Productivity, Not Efficiency'. Bain & Company. bain.com/insights/great-companies-obsess-over-productivity-hbr.

Lesson 10

Goldratt, Eliyahu M (1984). The Goal: A Process of Ongoing Improvement. North River Press.

Thaler, Richard H & Sunstein, Cass R (2009). *Nudge: Improving Decisions About Health, Wealth, and Happiness.* Penguin Books.

Chui, Michael et al. (2012). 'The social economy: Unlocking value and productivity through social technologies'. McKinsey Global Institute. mckinsey.com/industries/technology-media-and-telecommunications/our-insights/the-social-economy.

Lesson 11

Global Simplicity Index, simplicityindex.com.

Collinson, Simon (2012). 'Conquering complexity'. Public Finance. publicfinance.co.uk/2012/02/conquering-complexity.

Lesson 12

Sadun, Raffaella, Bloom, Nicholas & Van Reenen, John (2017). 'Why Do We Undervalue Competent Management?' *Harvard Business Review.* hbr.org/2017/09/why-do-we-undervalue-competent-management.

Flyvbjerg, Bent (2011). 'Over Budget, Over Time, Over and Over Again: Managing Major Projects' in Morris, Peter WG, Pinto, Jeffrey K & Söderlund, Jonas (eds.). *The Oxford Handbook of Project Management.* Oxford University Press.

Jenner, Steve (2014). *Managing Benefits.* The Stationery Office.

Wells, H. (2012). 'How effective are project management methodologies (PMMs)?: An explorative evaluation of their benefits in practice'. Paper presented at PMI® Research and Education Conference, Limerick, Munster, Ireland. Project Management Institute.

Heifetz, Ronald A & Linsky, Marty (2002). *Leadership on the Line: Staying Alive Through the Dangers of Leading.* Harvard Business Review Press.

McKeown, Greg (2014). *Essentialism: the disciplined pursuit of less.* Virgin Books.

McKay, Alicia (2019). *From Strategy to Action: A Guide to Getting Shit Done in The Public Sector.* Structured Conversations Ltd.

Business Wire (2016). 'PayPal Reports Strong Second Quarter Results and Raises Revenue Outlook'. businesswire.com/news/home/20160721006255/en/PayPal-Reports-Strong-Quarter-Results-Raises-Revenue.

Bruch, Heike & Ghoshal, Sumantra (2002). 'Beware the Busy Manager'. *Harvard Business Review.* hbr.org/2002/02/beware-the-busy-manager.

Garton, Eric & Mankins, Michael (2015). 'Engaging Your Employees Is Good, but Don't Stop There'. *Harvard Business Review*. hbr.org/2015/12/engaging-your-employees-is-good-but-dont-stop-there.

Heskett, James et al. (2008). 'Putting the Service-Profit Chain to Work'. *Harvard Business Review*. hbr.org/2008/07/putting-the-service-profit-chain-to-work.

Silvestro, Rhian (2014). 'Performance topology mapping: Understanding the drivers of performance.' *International Journal of Production Economics*. vol. 156, pp. 269–282.

Heath, Dan (2020). *Upstream: How to Solve Problems Before They Happen*. Bantam Press.

Lesson 13

Killingsworth, Matthew A & Gilbert, Daniel T (2010). 'A Wandering Mind is an Unhappy Mind'. *Science*, vol. 330.

Hollister, Rose & Watkins, Michael D (2018). 'Too Many Projects'. *Harvard Business Review*. hbr.org/2018/09/too-many-projects

Cloud, Henry (2011). *Necessary Endings: The Employees, Businesses, and Relationships That All of Us Have to Give Up in Order to Move Forward.* HarperCollins.

James, William (1890). *The Principles of Psychology.* Henry Holt and Company.

Lesson 14

Pressfield, Steven (2012). *Turning Pro: Tap Your Inner Power and Create Your Life's Work*. Black Irish Entertainment LLC.

McEachern, Sam (2020). 'How General Motors CEO Mary Barra Changed The Company's Dress Code For The Better'. GM Authority. gmauthority.com/blog/2020/06/

how-general-motors-ceo-mary-barra-changed-the-companys-dress-code-for-the-better.

Mintrom, Michael (2003). *People Skills for Policy Analysts.* Georgetown University Press.

Syed, Matthew (2019). Rebel Ideas: *The Power of Diverse Thinking.* John Murray.

Manhire, Toby (2020). 'Almost 90% of New Zealanders back Ardern government on Covid-19 – poll'. The Spinoff. thespinoff.co.nz/politics/08-04-2020/almost-90-of-new-zealanders-back-ardern-government-on-covid-19-poll.

Lesson 15

Wong, Kyle (2014). 'The Explosive Growth Of Influencer Marketing And What It Means For You'. Forbes. forbes.com/sites/kylewong/2014/09/10/the-explosive-growth-of-influencer-marketing-and-what-it-means-for-you/?sh=7a27e20852ac

Influencer Marketing Hub (2020). 'Digital Marketing and the Rise of the Micro Influencer'. influencermarketinghub.com/digital-marketing-and-the-rise-of-the-micro-influencer.

Innovisor (2017). 'How to Rethink Change with the Three Percent Rule'. innovisor.com/2017/05/30/how-to-rethink-change-with-the-three-percent-rule.

Chenoweth, Erica & Stephan, Maria J (2011). *Why Civil Resistance Works: Strategic Logic of Nonviolent Conflict.* Columbia University Press.

Urban, Erin (2017). 'What is your impact?'. Forbes. forbes.com/sites/forbescoachescouncil/2017/10/16/what-is-your-impact/?sh=25f4fea6f356.

Hatton, Shane Michael (2019). *Lead The Room: Communicate a message that counts in moments that matter.* Major Street Publishing.

Patterson, K et al. (2012). *Crucial conversations: tools for talking when the stakes are high.* Mcgraw-Hill.

Lieberman, Matthew (2015). *Social: Why Our Brains are Wired to Connect.* Oxford University Press.

Cuddy, Amy, Kohut, Matthew & Neffinger, John (2014). 'Connect, then lead.' *Harvard Business Review*, vol. 91, no. 7–8, pp. 54–61.

Pink, Daniel H (2012). *To Sell Is Human: The Surprising Truth About Moving Others.* Riverhead Books.

Sanders, Tim (2006). *The Likeability Factor: How to Boost Your L-Factor and Achieve Your Life's Dreams.* Crown.

Covey, Stephen M.R. (2006). *The Speed of Trust: why trust is the ultimate determinate of success or failure in your relationships, career and life.* Simon & Schuster.

Hansen, Jochim & Wänke, Michaela (2010). 'Truth From Language and Truth From Fit: The Impact of Linguistic Concreteness and Level of Construal on Subjective Truth'. *Personality and social psychology bulletin*, no. 36, pp. 1576–88.

Lesson 16

Church, Matt. mattchurch.com.

Lorenz-Spreen, P et al. (2019). 'Accelerating dynamics of collective attention'. *Nature Communications*, vol. 10.

Pink, Daniel H (2012). *To Sell Is Human: The Surprising Truth About Moving Others.* Riverhead Books.

Heath, Chip & Heath, Dan (2010). *Made to Stick: Why some ideas survive and others die.* Random House.

Pink, Daniel H (2011). *Drive: The Surprising Truth About What Motivates Us.* Penguin Putnam Inc.

Lieberman, Matthew D (2014). *Social: Why Our Brains Are Wired to Connect.* Broadway Books.

Godin, Seth (2008). *Tribes: We Need You to Lead Us.* Portfolio.

Where to from here?

Thompson, PM et al. (2000). 'Growth patterns in the developing brain detected by using continuum mechanical tensor maps'. *Nature*, vol. 204, pp. 190–193.

Clear, James (2018). *Atomic Habits: An easy and proven way to build good habits and break bad ones.* Avery.

INDEX

ACKNOWLEDGEMENTS

Writing a second book is a bit like having your second child. You go into it with a false sense of confidence, but once you're in the thick of it, you quickly remember how intense the whole thing is – and you've got to juggle the impact of your first effort at the same time!

None of this would have been possible without the support, inspiration and motivation of my biggest cheerleaders – my three daughters: Bailey, Charlotte and Harriet. Everything I do is fuelled by my desire to be a person that my children can be proud of. Girls, the world is your oyster. But it isn't perfect, so if you want to see it change, you'll have to do something about it – and I believe that you can.

I'm eternally grateful to the love and support of my wonderful friends – the family I've had the privilege of choosing. To my bestie Callum, I love you. On-call therapist, enthusiastic idea-bouncer, two-person dance party instigator and faithful run buddy, CV is the best friend I've ever known and without him, I'd be truly lost. Thanks for seeing me, friend.

To Wayne and Nikki, my siblings of sorts. Eighteen years of friendship, five children between us and a shared lifetime ahead. To Rachel, my partner in crime, a beautiful friend with a heart of gold. The womb of love, connection and support that comes from old friends must be one of the world's greatest treasures. I feel extremely lucky.

To Cam. For your love, patience and encouragement. For boundless hope, unavoidable growth, and the beautiful excitement of becoming.

To an incredible community of exceptional thinkers and friends – where would I be without you? To Digby, my incredible podcast co-host and valued friend, for keeping me laughing and thinking – even when I thought I'd run out of things to say. To Pete, for gently pulling my head in when I go off track and for your unconditional love and support.

A very special thanks to my clients, who made all of this possible by having faith in my ideas and giving me the freedom to make great things happen. Without all of you on board, I wouldn't know whether any of this actually… worked.

It's been a hell of a year. It's been a hell of a decade. There have been some epic highs, and some terrible lows, but I wouldn't change any of it. To all of those who've been an irreplaceable part of my journey, thank you. To Hamish, whose generosity, love and dedication ensure our children have a warm and safe core, and whose patience and friendship means I get to parent with the best father I know: I couldn't do any of this without you.

Finally, to all those who engage with my thinking, in person and online, attend my events, buy my books, share my ideas and give me something new to think about each and every day: thank you. This book is for you.

READY TO LEVEL UP?

For more help, check out **www.notanmba.co.nz** for free templates, tips and tools. To talk about partnering with me to level up the leaders in your organisation, head to **www.aliciamckay.co.nz**.

CONNECT WITH ME!

linkedin.com/in/aliciamckaynz
instagram.com/aliciamckaynz
facebook.com/aliciamckaynz

NOT AN MBA
A Leadership Programme Like No Other

For leaders serious about becoming more strategic – who don't have time for an MBA.

Not An MBA is a 20 week programme for aspiring and current leaders who want to cut the crap and learn meaningful skills they can use to make progress in a world gone mad. Using the five modules from *You Don't Need An MBA*, students take a deep dive into what it really means to be a strategic, adaptive leader in today's work environment.

Students access a world-class online curriculum, cutting-edge resources and a truly interactive and supportive learning environment with peers across the globe – plus direct access to Alicia McKay!

Not for the faint-hearted, Not An MBA is an intensive leadership programme that delivers serious results. All participants are expected to test and apply their learning, and prove their progress with their peers.

With two intakes every year, spots are strictly limited.

APPLY TO ENROL AT www.notanmba.co.nz